Gunnar Scott Reinbacher
Ole Preben Riis
Jörg Zeller, Eds.

THE CHALLENGE OF COMPLEXITY

AALBORG UNIVERSITY PRESS

The challenge of complexity
Gunnar Scott Reinbacher, Ole Preben Riis, Jörg Zeller, Eds.

Fourth volume in the series: Applied Philosophy / Anvendt Filosofi
1. edition
© Aalborg University Press, 2013

Painting on frontcover: Jörg Zeller
Layout of cover: akila v/ Kirsten Bach Larsen
Layout: akila v/ Kirsten Bach Larsen
Printed at AKA-PRINT 2013

ISBN: 978-87-7112-097-4
ISSN 2245-313X

Published by:
Aalborg University Press
Skjernvej 4A, 2nd floor
DK – 9220 Aalborg Ø
Phone: +4599407140
aauf@forlag.aau.dk
forlag.aau.dk

This book is published with financial support from Department of Learning and Philosophy, Aalborg University.

All rights reserved. No part of this book may be reprinted or reproduced or utilized in any form or by any electronic, mechanical, or other means, now known or hereafter invented, including photocopying and recording, or in any information storage or retrieval system, without permission in writing from the publishers, except for reviews and short excerpts in scholarly publications.

Contents

Jörg Zeller
    The Logic of complex problems and the various faces of complexity 5

Hans-Jörg Rheinberger
    An Experimental Systems Look on Complexity   15

Ole Preben Riis
    Sociology and Complexity   27

Michael Springer
    Physical Complexity   47

Lennart Nørreklit
    Complexity and practice control. On complexity and construct causality   59

Søren Willert
    The Natural History of Memory. An essay in complexity theory   87

Tina Maria Fussenegger
    From Static Cultures to Complex Societies. Complexity as an Ideological Tool of Description and Assessment   109

Jörg Zeller
    The complex logic of social work   123

List of authors   133

Jörg Zeller

The Logic of complex problems and the various faces of complexity

Complex things are either literally or metaphorically all-embracing or comprehensive. The word 'complex' is connected with the Latin verb 'complector' meaning – in its most literal sense – to embrace something or to hug someone. The substantive 'complexus' is thus originally an embracement or hug. In a more metaphorical sense a thing is complex if it comprehends a magnitude of homogeneous or different things. However, it depends of the kind of comprehension, if we conceive something that consists of many things as complex or not. It is perhaps most distinctive for complex phenomena that their properties and behavior aren't reducible to the properties and behavior of their elements. This poses some challenging metaphysical problems. Before I will engage in them I would like to make an epistemological detour and look at 'complexity' as a result of complicating action forms.

Temporarily philosophizing cognitive scientists (cf. Lakoff and Johnson 1999) claim that thinking – conceptual work – is metaphorical. Concepts, they say, are metaphors, i.e. translations or – in my understanding and more generally - transductions[1] from one universe of discourse and its on-

---

1 I understand by 'transduction' a widespread kind of inference that transfers or transduces given facts or conditions from one universe of discourse to another – like a ferry boat sailing people from one shore to another. For instance, the transformation of different kinds of physical energy into nerve energy is called transduction. Another example is of course the translation from one language into another. As a special kind of inferential thinking besides deduction, induction, and abduction, transduction can be understood as an *analogical* inference transferring (and transforming) knowledge

tology into another universe of discourse and ontology. This holds not at least for transductions from the tangible and concrete into the intangible and abstract. The tangible in tangible and not metaphoric sense presupposes a physical, spatio-temporal extended and energetically acted on and acting substance that can be grasped with one hand or both hands, be embraced or comprised with one arm or two arms and perhaps other parts of the body. To grasp or comprise something is, especially if it is performed consciously and intentionally, an action. If one in contrast tries to grasp or comprise something that can't be grasped or comprised in a tangible way then one does it metaphorically. In this case one doesn't any more act in a tangible, but in a metaphorical sense – one is thinking.

According to Piaget 1970 thinking is acting in this metaphorical sense. He called actions not with concrete, physically tangible objects but with representations, i.e. ideas or symbols of either objects or representations, *operations*. Ideas and symbols have that advantage over tangible objects that we without physical endeavor are able to carry them around and operate with them wherever we are and however it fits us. We are able to comprise them and form higher concepts, concepts of concepts so to say. We are, however, also able to dissolve them into subordinate concepts or conceptual components. And not least, operations on ideas or symbols are reversible – prototypal for instance arithmetical operations: to add and to subtract, to multiply and to divide.

Actions of this kind are either conceptually dissolving or analytic or they are conceptually composing or synthetic. Actions are events, i.e. transitions from an initial state to a final state. The initial state becomes by the action changed into the final state. The final state is the result of the action. In case of conceptual actions the result has a special form. Two or several concepts have been formed, i.e. embraced or comprised, into something new – into a conceptual connection called proposition. Because concepts are representations, propositions are also representations. While concepts represent individual objects (individual concepts[2]) or types of objects on the one hand and properties or relations,

---

from one universe of discourse to another, inhomogeneous one. In this transduction is in a similar way as abduction a knowledge amplifying or innovative inference mode.

2 I am aware of the objection to understand individuals as the result of conceptual work. As Frege 1892 made quite clear, the critical difference between concepts understood as object-types, properties or relations and individuals is the syntactic function as predicates of the former and as subjects of the latter. Notwithstanding this differ-

which can be used to identify or characterize objects, on the other hand, represent propositions states, events, processes, and actions.

Thinking can also be conceptually transferring or transducing actions – i.e. what we call inferences. There exist also here analytical – reductive or deductive – and synthetic – inductive, abductive or transductive – inference forms. Reductive thinking transduces compounds into their components, i.e. the more complex into the more simple. Inductive, abductive and transductive thinking expands more simple compounds into more complex ones. In short: thinking is conceptual actions of different complexity degrees. Or in other words: thinking consists in either complicating or – in contrast – simplifying concept-actions.

What have these logical trivialities to do with complexity problems in their ordinary ontological sense? Hitherto I have looked at complexity from a pragmatic point of view – as a result of complicating, embracing or comprehending actions or operations. Complex entities or phenomena attract, however, the attention of researchers on all reality levels – from physics to psychology and social sciences.

The study of complex phenomena is often understood in contrast to classical reductionist studies. The latter reduce complex phenomena to their most simple components and explain complexity as a deterministic result of an interaction of these components. Complex biological, social or communicative systems – for instance organisms, societies, Internet – have though emergent properties that can't be reduced to properties of their components. This too holds for all reality levels. A physically so simple substance as water has macroscopic properties – changing aggregate states at changing temperatures – that its molecules, atoms or elementary particles don't have on the microscopic level. This change of properties in the substantial fabrication of the real is a consequence of its complexity degree. Whatever it is the world ultimately consists of – it has an empirically realizable bias to generate more and more complex systems. It turns also out that the more complex these systems become the more unpredictable and uncontrollable they get, and the more im-

---

ence have predicative and individual concepts in common that both are results of comprising, comprehending and conceiving thinking-processes. We can't recognize or identify an individual object, say my cat Pollux, without comprising and comparing our different experiences made in different environments and under different conditions of the object. I can recognize Pollux again and again in different situations because I have formed a *concept*, i.e. a way to comprise, compare and conceive my different experiences of Pollux whenever I meet him or think of him.

possible they make their complete and final description. To find at least incomplete and preliminary descriptions you can, says the Belgian complexity scientist, Heylighen, use statistics, metaphors, simplifying models – also in form of computer simulations (cf. Heylighen 2008).

Before all this gets ontologically too complicated, let me epistemologically decelerate a bit and reflect the subject of my consideration from scratch. It makes still sense to divide phenomena and problems connected with them into complex and simple ones. Of course this is the case because complexity and simplicity, as I tried to sketch above, correspond our thinking mode. In a way, thinking is always 'complicating'. It comprehends and thus constructs or re-constructs compounds and thereby simplifies an informational and experiential chaotic and polydirectionally connected world. In other words, complexity and simplicity are connected with each other and make epistemologically sense.

The American physicist, Murray Gell-Mann 1997, has on this background created the term 'plektik', derived from the common Greek-Latin root, 'plektós', which asserts itself both in the word 'complex' and in the Latin word for 'simple', i.e. 'simplex'. The Greek 'plektós' means 'folded' or 'joint' – the Latin 'simplex' literally means 'folded once' or 'simple-minded'. By the way, the paradigm of cosmic evolution understood as a folding process asserts itself also in David Bohm's 1980/2007 concept of 'implicate order'. The paradigm, to say it quite simple-minded, boils down to the idea that the cosmic evolution with all its complexity degrees of system formation takes place as an implication or complication process. To understand this process, we have epistemologically to go the reverse way, i.e. unfold or explicate what there is in-folded or implicated in all those more or less complicated systems the world consists of.

However, one could wonder if – from an ontological point of view – speaking of simple objects, properties, relations, states or events, and systems of them makes sense at all. Contrary to the persistent metaphysical paradigm, saying that the world is a complex of complexes of simple entities, it is questionable which ontological status those simple entities, minimal objects – atoms or whatever we will call them – or alternatively minimal facts – original states or events or whatever we will call them – eventually should have. Whitehead 1984 says for instance:

> "Whenever we try to describe the object of our immediate experience, we realize that our understanding of it guides us beyond it

> to its contemporaneous, to its past, its future and to those universals by which its confinement is explained. But these universals incorporate just by their universality the possibility of other facts and alternative types of confinement. Of this reason the understanding of immediate, rough facts presupposes their metaphysical interpretation as aspects of a world that is systematically related to them." (ibidem: 51)

In other words, even if we with Wittgenstein's Tractatus-proposal shouldn't regard the world any more as a complex of elementary things or substances but instead of elementary facts then we aren't able to trace any simple facts as elements of the world either. In this case namely we meet intransparent causality problems. This noticed Leibniz already. In Monadology 36 he says about the sufficient reason of cases and facts understood as contingent and factual truths:

> "Here the dissolution into specific reasons could continue to the still more specific without limits because of the huge manifold of natural things and the infinite divisibility of bodies." (Leibniz 1967: 216, my transl.)

An ontologically unlimited complicated world results in unlimited complicated causal-nexus. A both substantially and causally unlimited complex and complicated world leaves two possibilities to us – either we have to be honest and abandon the idea that we ever could understand the world, i.e. become skeptics, or consider trying new ontologies and epistemologies. Considerations of this kind exist and can be associated with problems in non-linear systems. In linear systems, the effects are proportional to their causes; in non-linear systems effects aren't any longer proportional to their causes. Heylighen 2008 says:

> "The spreading of a wave is not a complex phenomenon, though, because its propagation is perfectly regular and predictable, and its strength diminishes as its reach widens. Processes in complex systems, on the other hand, are often non-linear: their effects are not proportional to their causes. When the effects are larger than the causes, we may say that there is an amplification or positive feedback: initially small perturbations reinforce themselves so as

> to become ever more intense. An example is the spread of a disease, where a single infection may eventually turn into a global pandemic. Another example is the chain reaction that leads to a nuclear explosion. When the effects are smaller than the causes, there is a dampening or negative feedback: perturbations are gradually suppressed, until the system returns to its equilibrium state." (ibidem: 4-5)

Perhaps the world is furnished both in a linear and non-linear way. It is regular as well as irregular, ordered an unordered, lawful and unlawful, and of the same reason predictable and unpredictable.

The suspicion that this is so isn't new at all. We know that it has in different guises challenged philosophers and scientists since the ancient roots of our modern science and research paradigms. Alarming is the idea, however, still for fundamentalists and determinists. With 'fundamentalism' and 'determinism' I mean here how the relationship between epistemology and ontology is understood. Fundamentalism boils down to the existence of original causes, determinism believes in compact chains of causes for every fact. The fundamentalist/determinist paradigm understands ontology as a hierarchic structure of entities unfolded as systems with different degrees of complexity and consisting of some irreducible, simple basic entities. The evolution of an ontologically complex world takes then in principle place by virtue of linear causality. The new entities and phenomena that apparently emerge in an evolutionary world has in one or other, but not always for us understandable, way been infolded in a primordial world layout. Emergent properties would for us be explainable in a linear way if we could dispose of more information about what's going on in the world. This information deficit is at the same time a consequence of our limited cognitive abilities constrained to spatiotemporal limited bodies.

The corresponding epistemology is, so to say, in a linear way connected with this ontology. We develop or construct – phylo- and ontogenetically – cognitive structures, i.e. concept, proposition, and inference structures and according methodologies that at least approximately correspond to determinist/fundamentalist ontology. Knowledge is a mental or symbolic map (isomorphism) or – in a more sophisticated variant – reconstruction of the ontology of the world. All our classic epistemological concepts like 'meaning', 'truth', and 'validity' are soaked by this ontological-epistemological linearity paradigm.

Could it be otherwise? Is a non-linear relation between epistemology and ontology conceivable? I would like to say yes. To give at least a sketch how I think it is conceivable I will go back to what I said in the beginning about the logic of complexity and the complexity of logic. By this I didn't mean that logic, i.e. our thinking or conceptual, propositional, and inferential acting is enormously complicated. Instead I tried to say that thinking in itself takes place in different forms of complicating and simplifying actions. I indicated also their non-linear character by saying that actions are processes of change, starting from initial conditions and resulting in the performed or produced change. If an action doesn't result in something else than it started from it doesn't succeed – it is not an action. If an understanding process doesn't amplify the knowledge we had in advance then it is not a knowledge creating and modifying process. Knowing is thus no linear transition from one knowledge state to another knowledge state. It is not just an acquisition of knowledge understood as being informed, it is an insight in the meaning and (value) consequences of this information.

The meaning and value(s) of something we are just able to realize and understand if we ourselves have generated this meaning and brought these values about. Action is in my opinion the bringing about (making real) of our thinking that on its part is to be understood as conceptualization (comprising, comparing, conceiving) of our experiences.

However, actions like everything else in the world don't take place in isolation but in complex connections with other actions and events in the world. I call action complexes practices. The difference between actions and events is that the former is governed by actors and intended, i.e. connected with an epistemology. As a consequence practices and their action components are value oriented. We act in order to realize what we believe is of value – for us and/or other people.

The following articles in this anthology don't follow a leitmotif – aside from that all of them have a look at complexity problems in different areas of scientific research. Hans-Jörg Rheinberger addresses complexity in the life sciences from the perspective of a historical epistemologist. He describes how complexity is handled by experimental model systems within molecular biology research.

Ole Preben Riis' essay represents – in his own words – "an attempt to indicate that a sociological stance can still be helpful for encounters with complex social problems. It concerns the practical application of social research rather than the pursuit of abstract knowledge about the complex social world we live in".

Michael Springer tries to explain the seemingly paradoxical fact how in physics complex models are used to reduce complex facts. This asserts for instance for "the macroscopic state of a system (that) 'emerges' from its microscopic state". "As far as the macroscopic quantities volume, pressure and temperature are concerned", Springer notices, "their emergence seems rather primitive: A vast number of micro-quantities are statistically compressed into three macro-quantities".

Lennart Nørreklit's "paper argues for a practice perspective" on the question: "What is the function of the concept (in casu complexity) in human construction of reality? What role does this concept play – not only in our understanding, but also in our doing, our living, i.e. in our way of organizing the practice of life?" The pivot of Nørreklit's considerations is the critical philosophical problem of action-causality or, as he calls it, 'construct-causality'.

Psychological research has notoriously to struggle with complexity problems. Søren Willert, both as a psychology practitioner and from a theoretical point of view, addresses problems of "natural historical continuity between the three ontological realms of (1) non-living (prebiotic) matter, (2) biosphere and (3) human life worlds respectively. This sense of continuity contrasted sharply with a physicalist world view. Physicalism poses an absolute discontinuity between pre-biotic matter and biosphere, thereby making the transition from non-living matter to biosphere an enigma". Looking at the "natural history of memory" Willert is searching for ways how to bridge the complexity gaps between the different levels of evolution.

The aim of Tina Maria Fussenegger's "essay is … to introduce some of the different points of view, which have contributed to the definitions and clarification processes of complexity" in social anthropology research. The complexity to be handled in this research concerns questions of social and cultural evolution. This is according to Fussenegger so because "the human world can be imagined as a place, where every action someone takes will influence the life of someone else".

Jörg Zeller considers in his article how "the complex problems of social work as a profession – to help another person to become able to realize a good life – can be solved". He thinks "inspiration can be found in Wittgenstein's idea – or rather method – of language games". The reason why the concept of language game is applicable as an appropriate method to tackle the complex logic of social work is according to Zeller that the logic of language games is based on the fact "that the meaning and value of those things and instruments the interacting participants" in a social work situation "use and manipulate is not determined in advance but result of the interaction of all parts – conscious and unconscious – of the interaction".

References

Frege Gottlob 1892, Über Begriff und Gegenstand, in: Frege G. 1967, Kleine Schriften, Darmstadt: Wissenschaftliche Buchgesellschaft, p. 167-178.

Heylighen Francis 2008, Complexity and Self-Organisation, in: Bates M. J. and Maack M. N. eds. 2008, Encyclopedia of Library and Information Sciences, London and New York: Taylor & Francis.

Lakoff George and Johnson Mark 1999, Philosophy in the Flesh, New York: Basic Books.

Leibniz Gottfried Wilhelm 1956, Monadologie, in: Leibniz G. W. 1956, Vernunftprinzipien der Natur und der Gnade; Monadologie, Hamburg: Felix Meiner Verlag, p. 26-69.

Piaget Jean 1970, Genetic Epistemology, New York and London: Columbia University Press.

Hans-Jörg Rheinberger

An Experimental Systems Look on Complexity[1]

The following remarks on experimental model systems and complexity in the life sciences are those of a historical epistemologist. I am speaking neither as a theoretical biologist nor as a philosopher of biology. I understand historical epistemology to be a reflection of the practical as well as theoretical, material as well as conceptual, scientific as well as cultural *conditions* of knowledge acquisition in their historical entrenchment. I came to be introduced to molecular biology in the late 1970s, and I have experienced it as a largely *empirical* culture heavily relying on lab work systems. My historical and epistemological remarks carry the mark of this enculturation.

An anecdote might help to set the stage. About twenty-five years ago, I visited one of Berkeley's foremost molecular biologists, Gunther Stent, who was then spending some time as a fellow at the Institute for Advanced Study in Berlin. We had lunch together and he asked me what I was doing. I told him that, besides doing experiments on in vitro protein biosynthesis, I was working on the history of evolutionary theory, in particular on the theory of selection. "But 'selection' is no longer a theory," he invoked. "Selection is a process that can be produced and manipulated in

---

1 This is a slightly amended version of the following paper: Hans-Jörg Rheinberger, Experimental model systems. An epistemological aperçu from the perspective of molecular biology. In: Manfred D. Laublicher and Gerd B. Müller (eds.), Modeling Biology. Structures, Behaviors, Evolution. MIT Press, Cambridge MA 2007, pp. 37-45. I wish to thank the Press and the editors for the permission of reproducing it with appropriate changes.

the laboratory." During the long and heated debate that followed he stuck to his claim that science, in the end, is not an activity that leads to entities such as theories but, just the other way round, it is an activity that ultimately resolves theories into something for which there is a very appropriate old German word: a *Sachverhalt*, that is, a relation between things. For Stent, theory was something speculative that bridged gaps. If the gaps disappeared, so did the need for the bridges. In this discussion, Stent certainly played the role of a devil's advocate (he was one of the most intellectually minded early molecular biologists), but his statement intrigued me, and it has continued to intrigue me ever since. To put it in other terms: The claim is that the apotheosis and, ultimately, the fulfillment of a theory is its dissolution.

If it is not a theoretical framework in the first place, how is molecular biology to be addressed? We can look at it as a network of more-or-less articulated experimental systems evolving around scientific objects that enter into more-or-less specified relations to one another. I will use the notion of experimental system, model system, or experimental model system synonymously, as scientists do when they talk about their work.

There can be no doubt that the objects of molecular biological research are physico-chemical entities. In its deliberate search for the physico-chemical basis of life, molecular biology has frequently been criticized and accused of driving reductionism to its extremes. But it is precisely in following such a reductive modeling strategy that molecular biology has been confronted with an obstacle from within, namely, that these physico-chemical objects exhibit quite singular and historically unique structures that are, as products of evolution, physico-chemically possible, but not physico-chemically necessary. Just to mention one fundamental example: At least as far as can be said today, there appears to be no possibility to deduce the particular letters of the genetic code, that is, to assign a particular nucleic acid triplet to a particular amino acid, on the sole basis of stereo-chemical principles. Obviously, we have to do here with historical contingencies, a 'frozen accident' as it was, that are the product of evolution and are only accessible to an analysis of empirical detail. They cannot be deduced from first principles. Michael Polanyi concluded from this fact very early on that the objects of biology in this sense are categorically distinct from the objects of the other sciences (Polanyi 1969). A number of years ago, Richard Burian remarked, and I think rightly so from the point of view adopted here, that historical contingency is probably the deepest reason for the overwhelming importance of empirical research in virtually all disciplines of modern biology (Burian 1995). Of molecular biology in particular, Burian even claimed that it looks more like a battery of techniques than a general theory. If not a mere battery of techniques, an articulated ensemble of experimental systems: this is the view taken here. Finding appropriate model systems appears then to be the only way to do productive research in this situation.

A short look at the history of elucidating the genetic code between 1953 and 1963 is indeed revealing in this respect. If we follow Lily Kay's historical analysis (Kay 2000), all efforts of theoretical physicists after the establishment of the structure of the double helix to deduce the code from a priori considerations failed: George Gamow's, Francis Crick's, Henry Quastler's, and those of many others. It was only nearly a decade later, in 1961, that a biochemical model system of in vitro protein synthesis, originally set up for reasons even unrelated to molecular biology, entered the scene of experimental molecular genetics. To the disappointment of all those who had so desperately been racking their brains over coding rules, the code was solved on the basis of an empirical assay. None of those who finally managed to do the job – Heinrich Matthaei, Marshall Nirenberg, and all the others thereafter – had been involved in the painstaking theoretical speculations that preceded this experimental feat, and the other way round, all those involved in the early speculations were left behind.

On the level of conceptualization, things do not look very different. When conducting a historical analysis concerning the introduction of the notion of information in the scientific papers of the French molecular biologists François Jacob and Jacques Monod (Rheinberger 2006), the analysis led me to the conclusion that the sequence of papers shows no sharply defined conceptual break. Instead, different layers of notions were successively added to form a genuinely hybrid discourse. The initial, explicitly structural vocabulary of specificity and determination was first supplemented by a performative vocabulary of prescription, execution, and control which was taken over – in the case of Jacob and Monod - from the study of lysogeny and the induction of lactose metabolism in *Escherichia coli*. To this already hybrid discourse was then added the language of information, message, and code, thereafter the language of communication and signaling, and finally the language of reading and writing a text. All these language layers carried along with them quite different conceptualizations. These different idioms did not replace each other in clearly separated steps, and they were not used as clearly distinct model conceptions. They came to coexist with each other. They became superimposed upon each other and supplemented each other as different registers of one single experimental model system which was itself a hybrid system combining the study of sugar metabolism and viral gene transfer in the bacterium *E. coli*. These registers allowed for very subtle modulations of the system. They remind us of the fact that the language in which an experimental science expresses its results develops in tight connection with the technical means and media of realizing and developing the experimental systems on which the science relies and on whose outcomes the further avenues of research depend. The notion of information in particular became only slowly part and parcel of that patchy discursive network. And it is not by chance that it never took on the technical, purely quantitative meaning bestowed on it by information theory. "Information" instead occupied the place of historically preceding versions of biological specificity. It took on the meaning of a representation of the structural repository of biological function.

"The living world is one of complexity, the result of innumerable interactions among organisms, cells, molecules. In analyzing a problem, the biologist is constrained to focus on a fragment of reality, on a piece of the universe which he arbitrarily isolates to define certain of its parameters. In biology, any study thus begins with the choice of a 'system'" (Jacob 1988: 234). What transpires through these words, taken from the autobiography of François Jacob, is the conviction that, because of the very conditions of possibility of biological experience and knowledge acquisition, the fragmentation of reality, the cutting of the universe of the living into pieces is a prerequisite for the constitution of biological knowledge. Jacob held that although there are generalizations in biology that can go further or less far at times, there are very few, if any, theories (Jacob 1974). We might well claim with the historian of biology, Georges Canguilhem, that for most cases in the history of biology *concepts* rather than theories have been the organizing centers. And if we follow Stent in addition, the successful ones among them interact and become amalgamated with particular scientific objects that can be manipulated in experimental systems. Canguilhem has concluded from this that the history of biology is best written as a history of concepts.

Consequently, what we need on the epistemological level, is, as I have argued in my book *Toward a History of Epistemic Things* (Rheinberger

1997), in following the French epistemologist Gaston Bachelard, a "philosophy of the epistemological detail" (Bachelard 1966). Philosophers have often seen such fragmentation as a deplorable, albeit possibly inescapable limitation of empirical knowledge. We can view it, however, quite differently. With Bachelard, I would rather contend that this imagined limit is a condition of the possibility for empirically grounded scientific knowledge expansion. Science, in the sense of the word we have become acquainted with, is a way of gaining *unprecedented*, that is, *new* knowledge. For this to happen, conditions must be created that, in contrast to deductive systems, allow for epistemic events that *cannot* be anticipated.

Experimental systems appear precisely as the arrangements that allow for the creation of cognitive, spatio-temporal singularities and thus, for the coming about of unprecedented epistemic events. The attentive study of experimental systems in molecular biology and the networks they constitute leads to the realization that these systems are thus, according to the words of Jacob once again, "machines for making the future" (Jacob 1988: 9). They are instances of iteration, of differential reproduction in the realm of empirical knowledge acquisition. A history of molecular biology in particular will have much to contribute to such an epistemology of iteration, exactly because of the eminently patch-worked structure of its practices entrenched in experimental systems. In order to understand this broader epistemic network, we need to understand, in the words of the Belgian philosopher Isabelle Stengers, the material as well as the conceptual "operations of propagation" and "operations of passage" that shape such networks into more-or-less cohesive fields of knowledge production (Stengers 1987).

Powerful experimental systems must be located—quite literally—at the cutting edge of the fractionation process just described. They operate most productively at the fluctuating, unstable boundary between the trivial and the complex. For a particular experimental system, however partial or reduced, the broader network represents complexity as a kind of 'epistemic horizon.' Within a particular experimental system, the tendency to experimental reduction of complexity prevails. There are no general rules that guarantee that these reductive moves proceed in directions that are being accepted in the long run and contribute to the overall picture. In the end, it is the network of experimental systems itself that decides about the epistemic value of its elements. If, as we may take for granted, ontic complexity *has* to be reduced in order to make experimental research possible and experimental systems work, the essential complexity of the living is epistemically retained and constantly reconstituted and reconfigured in the rich contexture of an experimental landscape, in which new connections and disconnections between model systems can happen at any time, and where the eruption of one 'volcanic system' can change the whole landscape around it, through passage and through propagation.

With concepts such as conjuncture, hybridization, and ramification, I have tried to capture some relations within ensembles of experimental systems and their intricate interactions (Rheinberger 1997: Ch. 9). These concepts express a vision of a structure of articulated experimental networks of objects and practices whose coherence, just as in the case of individual experimental systems, is patched and whose meaningfulness is due to lateral constitution, to horizontal concatenation. The cohesion of the systems reaches as far as epistemic entities may circulate throughout the network. Conjunctures, hybridizations, and ramifications describe the dynamics of reorientation, fusion, and proliferation of particular experimental systems in terms of shifts, links, and descent. These processes translate the microdynamics of localized and situated experimental systems into the mesodynamics of the broader, surrounding fields of experimentation.

With this, we come very near to an idea of Stuart Kauffman he calls the patch procedure. "The basic idea of the patch procedure is simple: take a hard, conflict-laden task in which many parts interact, and divide it into a quilt of non-overlapping patches. Try to optimize within each patch. As this occurs, the couplings between parts in two patches across patch boundaries will mean that finding a 'good' solution in one patch will change the problem to be solved by the part in the adjacent patches. Since changes in each patch will alter the problems confronted by the neighbouring patches, and the adaptive moves by those patches in turn will alter the problem faced by yet other patches, the system is just like our model coevolving ecosystems. [...] We are about to see that if the entire conflict-laden task is broken into the properly chosen patches, the coevolving system lies at a phase transition between order and chaos and rapidly finds very good solutions. Patches, in short, may be a fundamental process we have evolved in our social systems, and perhaps elsewhere, to solve very hard problems" (Kauffman 1995).

Applied to experimental model systems, we may call this the patchwork view of research. It leads us to look for a logic that is neither exhausted by the rationality of individual actors nor by the social conventions of a broader discipline. With that, it lies somewhere between the extremes of Cartesian egos and Kuhnian paradigms that for so long have dominated philosophy and history of science. Patchwork epistemology is the quest for conceptual tools that may help to clarify a little better the historical evolution of the sciences and to understand how we can have both: reductive experimentation and an understanding of complex processes both in nature and in gaining knowledge about nature.

In his encompassing conceptual history of biology, *The Growth of Biological Thought*, published in 1982, Ernst Mayr devoted only the last chapter to molecular biology (Mayr 1982). While praising its technical breakthroughs, he considered it of minor impact with regard to the great conceptual challenges of biology which he thought had basically been solved, and of course, solved by the synthesis of evolutionary theory and classical genetics. Mayr was right and he was not. He was right in that molecular biology started as a technical, physico-chemical conquest. It was not a readymade notion of genetic information that guided molecular biology's efforts from the beginning. Rather, conceiving of biological specificity in a new way diffused slowly – as I have tried to show – into the partial systems of the new biology. And for quite a while, molecular biology appeared to live happily with a gene concept, for instance, that was in no way hurting the claims of classical genetics. By pinning the gene down to DNA, molecular biology simply appeared to add a material, molecular dimension to it, and to open a new field of experimentation: bacterial and phage genetics.

But Mayr was also wrong, because the situation also profoundly changed along the way. And yet, the quite radical changes that the views of biological specificity and of genes and genome structures have undergone in the course of the past fifty years or so are by no means the result of deliberately alternative approaches called onto the scene in order to counteract reductionist genetics and molecular biology. On the contrary, local experimental sophistication with experimental models, reaching down to the molecular level as a kind of obligatory passage point, exploded a rather coarse and simplistic – judged from hindsight - gene concept deeply from within molecular biology. As a result, it led to quite unprecedented vistas that are sometimes subsumed under the label of a 'clever genome.' A whole battery of mechanisms and entities has been identified - often by exploiting the tools of gene technology -

that constitute what could be called a system of hereditary 'respiration' (Rheinberger 2000). It is the complexities of the hereditary system that are now more and more fore-grounded and more and more seen in their interaction with the complexities of the phenotype. Evolutionary developmental biology has become the catchword (See, e.g., Laubichler & Maienschein 2007).

During the past thirty years or so, we have witnessed a resurgence of developmental biology as it was forced through the bottleneck of molecular genetics. The work of Christiane Nüsslein-Vollhard, Ed Lewis, Eric Wieschaus, Walter Gehring, and others on the homeobox system and on many other regulatory master switches in early development has brought long-elusive morphological patterns into the realm of molecular interpretation. Developmental biology had been widely set aside by classical transmission genetics since the 1920s, and by early molecular biology as well. Yet, here again, it was neither an alternative organismic approach nor a re-evaluation of earlier developmental theories that paved the way to new vistas on "homology" and to what now is called the "zootype." It was rather the intelligent exploitation of a set of new techniques belonging to genetic engineering that helped to open the box again. With a lengthy quote from the book of John Maynard Smith and Eörs Szathmáry about the *Major Transitions in Evolution* I come back to my initial considerations: "There are some profound consequences of this definition of animals. The zootype is based on functions that are informational: it is easy to imagine that different systems could have evolved in different phyla. Thus the organization of the zootype is gratuitous, and indicates common ancestry, rather than convergent adaptation or developmental constraints. [...] This observation is a rather strong blow at the essentialist or structuralist approach to body plans: the definition of animals rests on genetic ancestry, rather than on first principles of form." And they go on: "How can we expect to gain further insight? The best hope lies in molecular genetics. Molecular data are the main reason for accepting the monophyletic origin of metazoans. The homeobox story [...] tells us that the common ancestor of the chordates and the arthropods probably already had a differentiated head, middle and tail. The regulatory genes responsible for the differentiation were already present. Since their DNA-binding region, the homeobox, is also present in the gene-determining mating type in yeast, it is likely that the common ancestor of these genes already existed in their protist ancestor. No-one could have foreseen these observations. We can reasonably hope that future discoveries will be equally illuminating" (Maynard Smith & Szathmáry 1995: 254, 224).

At a conference on "Rethinking the Enlightenment" a number of years ago, the historian of science Yehuda Elkana asked the rhetorical question whether the time was ripe for challenging and daring alternatives in the sciences, or whether we needed to do just more of the same. My equally rhetorical answer to this perennial question is that we need to do more of the same *precisely* in order to arrive at unprecedented alternatives. The only *fruitful* and lasting way to reach out beyond the confines of a system, in particular of any model system, is to try hard to explore its limits and finally to transform or even founder it from within.

At the end of *At Home in the Universe,* Kauffman ponders: "I wonder if we really understand very much of what we are creating." And he continues: "All we can do is to be locally wise, even though our own best efforts will ultimately create the conditions that lead to our transformations to utterly unforeseeable ways of being" (Kauffman 1995: 298, 303). Local wisdom is what characterizes the practices of an endeavor that, since the Enlightenment and contrary to all appearance and experience, never ceased to depict itself as an allegedly global undertaking: the making of 'Science.' I contend that the order of the day for epistemology is learning to understand how local wisdoms, embedded in research attractors such as experimental systems, get connected to knowledge patchworks, to ever new and changing configurations of niches of knowing. Fragmentation – "cantonization" in the language of Bachelard (Bachelard 1949: 103) – far from being deficient, deleterious, and deplorable, then must appear as one of the basic conditions of unprecedented development.

Understanding the experimental dynamics that lie behind these transformations of our views on development and evolution is what a "philosophy of the epistemological detail" in the sense of Bachelard has to address. This does not of course amount to theoretical biology, nor is it philosophy of biology from an ontological perspective. If anything, these considerations are meant to contribute elements to a theory, or philosophy, *about* the constitution of biology as a science. Within this *epistemological* context, I have argued, experimental model systems play a major role. If I for my part may draw a conclusion, it is the following: Historical epistemology, too, must become quasi molecular and experimental if it wants to live up to the scientific practices it tries to analyze and understand. Well-selected case studies are its model systems, then. Such an endeavour has begun, but there is certainly still a long way to go in this direction.

References

Bachelard, Gaston 1949, *Le rationalisme appliqué*, Paris: Presses Universitaires de France.

——— 1966 [1940], *La philosophie du non*, Paris: Presses Universitaires de France.

Burian, Richard 1995, What is this science we have made? Some epistemological issues regarding molecular biology, Manuscript.

Jacob, François 1974, Le modèle linguistique en biologie, *Critique*, 322: 197-205.

——— 1988, *The Statue Within. An Autobiography*, New York: Basic Books.

Kauffman, Stuart A. 1995, *At Home in the Universe. The Search for Laws of Self-Organization and Complexity*, Oxford: Oxford University Press.

Kay, Lily E. 2000, *What is the Book of Life? A History of the Genetic Code*, Stanford: Stanford University Press.

Laubichler, Manfred D. and Jane Maienschein, eds. 2007, *From Embryology to Evo-Devo: A History of Developmental Evolution*, Cambridge MA: MIT Press.

Maynard Smith, John and Eörs Szathmáry 1995, *The Major Transitions in Evolution*, New York: W. H. Freeman.

Mayr, Ernst 1982, *The Growth of Biological Thought: Diversity, Evolution, and Inheritance*, Cambridge (MA): Harvard University Press.

Polanyi, Michael 1969, Life's irreducible structure. In: Polanyi, Michael, Marjorie Green, eds. 1969, *Knowing and Being. Essays*, Chicago: The University of Chicago Press.

Rheinberger, Hans-Jörg 1997, *Toward a History of Epistemic Things. Synthesizing Proteins in the Test Tube*, Stanford: Stanford University Press.

——— 2000, Gene concepts. Fragments from the perspective of molecular biology. In: Beurton, Peter, Raphael Falk and Hans-Jörg Rheinberger (eds.). *The Concept of the Gene in Development and Evolution*, pp. 219-239, Cambridge: Cambridge University Press.

——— 2006, The notions of regulation, information, and language in the writings of François Jacob 2006, *Biological Theory*, 1: 261-267.

Stengers, Isabelle 1987, La propagation des concepts. In: Stengers, Isabelle (ed.). *D'une science à l'autre. Des concepts nomades*. Paris: Seuil.

Ole Preben Riis

Sociology and Complexity

Introduction

Sociology was originally launched at the time of the French Revolution as an attempt to produce a general theory of industrial society. It was supposed to integrate knowledge from other social sciences, including social history, law, economics, statistics, political science and so forth. However, sociology has become another subdiscipline, which focuses on a specific set of problems. We know that social life depends on nature, the weather, geography, physiology et cetera. We know that our interpretation of social life depends on culture, such as the dynamic associative figurations of language. We know that confrontations with social problems depend on historical memories. Sociological theories affirm that the social world we participate in is becoming increasingly complex. Theories concerning globalization, network society or the world system address the complexity of late modern society at a macro level. However, most sociological studies seem to focus on non-complex issues which operate at a meso- or microlevel. Most sociological studies seem to form a separated agenda which brackets economic, legal or political aspects of the problem. This thematic insulation is common in academia. By focusing on their own agenda, the challenge of complexity is ignored. However, in the real social world, complexity becomes an ever-increasing challenge. This essay represents an attempt to indicate that a sociological stance can still be helpful for encounters with complex social problems. It concerns the practical application of social research rather than the pursuit of abstract knowledge about the complex social world we live in. This point has a personal side: I was for five years employed as a planning consultant at the architect firm Møller and Grønborg, and the inspiration and learning from that period has a deep impact on my later work as university sociologist. The example discussed below is the Danish debate on 'ghettoization'. This reflects on some of the tasks I was allowed to work on as consultant for Møller and Grønborg and other employers – such as the 1981 report on the squatter township of Christiania in Copenhagen (Møller & Grønborg 1981). So this essay can also be read as a biographical reflexion.

1. Encounters with Complexity

Imagine that you are suddenly placed in a society which is organized in a manner entirely different from that in your own society. You can observe that people are acting in a manner which seems purposeful and co-ordinated. But you do not know the rules yet. There are many signs which indicate directions or guidance, but you do not know the language. You can identify institutions and roles, but do not know their meaning. The encounter is confusing, exciting and also a source for anguish. Some people react by retreating to islands which resemble their own society, at least on the surface.

Tokyo represents a complex co-ordination of the lives of millions of people in a relatively small space. Their everyday lives are to be connected in predictable manners. People commute between home and work-place and service-centres. They seem to know the intricate set of rules which regulate and coordinate their lives. However, these rules are difficult to explain to foreigners. They are taken for granted and even small children know them. For instance, that you always walk to the left, in a smooth manner so that other people do not bump into you. That you do not claim much space, in order to let other people have sufficient space. That you demonstrate politeness and gratitude to all people, who service you, including the toilet cleaner at the subway station, and the customers who grace your shop by their visit.

Social life in this complex society seems like a ballet where all dance their parts to an unnoticed music. This coordinated pattern may be ripped up by idiots or strangers who do not recognize their parts. People, who do not take place in the queue, who push others and talk loudly in the subway so that other people cannot stand up and sleep in a strap. These strangers cross the invisible lines. They embarrass you and make you feel unbalanced and insecure. They are therefore to be avoided, ignored and shunned. Unless, of course, they show respect and acknowledge their oddity.

Tokyo represents a very advanced way of organizing society. It depends on socializing the social agents to a set of values and rules, most of which are not formalized. A volume which describes the values, the hidden rules and assumptions would be very large. Guidance for children is a good place to begin. Another cue is the questions Japanese ask strangers about their (our) odd manners. These questions are very polite, of course, but they reveal wonder about our social behavior and our society. Such questions may be difficult to answer for a visitor from Europe, because we hardly think about the ways our society operates. We take the system and its regulation for granted. Complexity emerges as we have to explain how the social system operates and how we adapt to its written and hidden rules. We often first notice these hidden rules when we visit societies where they are out of order – like in parts of Southern Europe – or exchanged with another set of rules.

What I have tried to outline here is social complexity, in the dual meaning that late modern society is complex by involving many people and many organizations, and that our perceptual model of this society is also complex. Our perceptual model forms late modern society, but it does not always function according to the model. Late modern society contains dynamics which do not follow expectations by the model. This may lead to efforts to control the dynamic and also reformulation of the model. In order to function as individuals or organizations, we need to have a perceptual model of the society we operate in. Our perceptual model is both a model of and for society; it describes and it forms what it describes but not always in the intended or expected manner. Social theory represents abstract maps which outline parts of the perceptual model of society. Such theories cannot and should not depict actual society with all its details. Theories reduce the complexity of social life, as maps which produce an overview of some features which can be relevant for our operating in society. Maps are not pictures, but simplified and selective descriptions. Social theories not only describe, they also interpret and explain, and thereby resemble manuals. They indicate some general rules for operation in society. As long as we consider the processes in singularity, it is relatively easy to handle them. However, with social complexity, more processes are connected with each other. To initiate one process has implications for several other processes, which have feedbacks on the first process. Thus, the manual cannot just describe each operation but must consider its connection to other operations.

The encounter with Tokyo represents perceiving a social situation which is highly regulated, but where you do not know the rules. Encounters with chaotic situations are different in character. Chaotic situations are unpredictable, whereas complex situations are in principle predictable – but you have not deciphered the regulating rules. Encounter with chaos leads to high stress, because you have to be prepared for all possibilities. Chaotic situations are therefore avoided. When you enter a new social territory, it may at first seem chaotic. However, further observations indicate that there are nevertheless some regulating rules. For instance, tourists who visit the free-town of Christiania in Copenhagen for the first time may find it quite chaotic. However, a more thorough sociological study will reveal that life in Christiania is regulated by internal norms. These are not identical with the norms in other parts of Copenhagen, and they are not formalized or explicit. The norms are regularly trespassed, challenged and contested. Nevertheless, you are able to identify a set of norms which can direct your actions.

In a similar, but much more dramatic way, the shanty towns in the developing world may at first seem chaotic. In Mathare Valley at Nairobi, uniformed representatives of the social order are normally conspicuously absent. The mud huts seem haphazard and behavior seems unpredictable. Nevertheless, when you get close enough, it becomes evident that social life is regulated. Because people live on so few resources, and under a potential dread, they are very attentive to ways in which they can cope and protect themselves and their fellows.

The following discussion first addresses questions about the relation between epistemology and theory relating to complex social issues, and then takes up the debates about ghettoization in the fall of 2010 as an example, in order to discuss how social theory could contribute to address aspects of this type of complex social problems.

2. Complex Social Theory

We have come to realize that the world we live in is more complex than assumed by former generations. We have obtained a more facetted knowledge about our physical world; and we have become citizens of a global world society which is more complex than even the large historical empires. As participants in an interdependent economic world system, and as participants in a global communicative network, we are confronted with complex challenges. A tsunami at the coast of Japan has an impact on our life, at the opposite part of the hemisphere; the domestic market across the Atlantic has an impact on our financial situation.

In a 'post-industrial' society (Bell 1976), research is considered as a vital form of capital which is needed in order to develop and produce new types of commodities. Corporations calculate investments in production of knowledge and estimate their capitalized value. Governments focus increasingly on research and development, and try in different ways to stimulate, measure and control it. Research has become a central institution in society which is allotted many resources but is also increasingly held responsible for its utility.

Public means have increasingly been assigned to research on what we may call 'complex problems'. These refer to challenges which necessitate a multi-dimensional, multi-disciplinary approach. Complexity is in the present discussion regarded as a relative position on a scale which goes from simple unidimensional reductionism on the one hand to chaotic holism on the other. Complexity thus refers to an attempt to reduce a problem to as few dimensions as possible and as many as necessary for analyzing and handling it. This represents a pragmatic approach to complexity which may be challenged. There is no fixed answer to how many dimensions are needed. The answer changes as we obtain more knowledge about the problem and begin to use our knowledge for solving parts of it. The presented problems are not fixed as classical theses. Complex problems are like open systems, where the processes are influenced by our changing definition of the problem, our attitude to it, our motives to solve it, our knowledge about solutions and their side-effects, material conditions and mechanisms which influence the processes.

Social theories typically avoid the challenge of complexity by abstraction or differentiation. Abstract theories admit the complexity but render models which are difficult to operate by. Differentiated theories select a few dimensions in a manner which can be operationalized, but disregard their relation to the complex framework. Academia is subject to a centrifugal process of differentiation, where an increased production of knowledge corresponds with an increasing fragmentation of types of knowledge. Efforts to integrate knowledge across disciplines are generally regarded as superficial and suspect by the established disciplines – with some good reasons.

There is, however, a discrepancy between this centrifugal process and demands in society for knowledge about complex social problems. These demands can be illuminated by ear-marked project funds which call for inter-disciplinary or trans-disciplinary research. The problem of addressing complex problems is not only one of funding but also one of organization and communication. In former times, philosophy represented an attempt to integrate the fragments of knowledge. However, in present academia, philosophy tends to become another specialized discipline. Positivism was carried by a vision of a unified science. However, in present academia, knowledge is pursued more by autonomous disciplines pursuing their separate agendas, rather than by attempts to form meaningful integrated interpretations of the increasing heap of fragmented information.

Complex social phenomena depend on interrelations between several dimensions, including natural, cultural and social ones. In order to contribute to illuminate complex problems, sociology has to acknowledge its relation to other fields of research and it must develop theories which are open to analytical dimensions beyond its scope of competence.

3. The Danish Debate on Ghettoization

One of the major themes in the political debate during the fall of 2010 concerned ghettoization. It is a recurrent theme. Ghettoization refers to a concentration of a complex of social problems in a limited district: some social housing areas are statistically prone to a constellation of relatively many inhabitants with low income, low education, high unemployment rates, high crime rates, high rates of immigrants or descendents of immigrants, et cetera. The following analysis aims to indicate how the complexity of the problem is approached from different parties.

In October 2010, the Liberal-Conservative government presented a plan aiming 'to bring the ghettos back to society'. The plan states that the government cannot tolerate the development of 'a parallel society' characterized by its own values. Danish society is generally characterized as free, safe and affluent. It is carried by a set of values which include freedom to differ, equal opportunities for men and women, shared responsibility for society, democracy, respect for the laws of society, and a basic trust that we wish each other well. The core of the ghetto complex is thus identified as value-based. The ghettos are described as pursuing itheir own set of values which deviate from Danish values in general and this leads to their social and cultural insulation. This approach to the complex problem follows a major agenda by the Liberal-Conservative government which has ruled Denmark since 2001 supported by the populist right-wing party, namely an effort to re-establish Danish values under the threat of multiculturalism and especially Muslim immigration.

Ghetto areas are characterized by: 1) a high proportion of inhabitants who are neither employed nor under education; 2) a high proportion of immigrants or descendents of immigrants from non-Western countries; 3) a high proportion of inhabitants convicted for crimes. As a solution, the government proposes that the housing areas shall not be isolated from the rest of society; that more inhabitants shall be employed or under education; that the criminal behavior shall be stopped; that the high concentration of immigrants from non-Western countries shall be reduced. These are decisive for a genuine integration, according to the government.

The initiative seems to approach ghettoization as a complex problem, involving employment, ethnicity, crime, and social trust. It further tries to identify a core problem within the complex, namely deviant values. However, the government's plan does not indicate how the dimensions of the complex are connected, and how they are derived from the value dimension. It does not provide any documentation for the claim about deviant values. The plan assumes that those who inhabit the ghettos do it by their own choice in order to live according to a deviant set of values. The plan does not document that the ghetto inhabitants actually pursue deviant values. It is theoretically possible that they share the described values, but are hindered to pursue them in their everyday life for practical reasons, that they hold several different sets of values, or that they are anomic in the sense that they regard values as abstract ideals without any practical relevance for everyday survival.

The initiatives include 1) a reduction in the number of social housing; 2) to dissolve the physical isolation of the areas and make them more attractive and integrated with the surrounding society; 3) to regulate movement into the areas (which has hitherto been regulated by the cooperative ownership); 4) to improve the Danish skills of the children; 5) to bring those inhabitants on social security into jobs or education; 6) to strengthen police in the areas and supervise social fraud and thereby restore respect for the laws of society; 6) a co-ordinated effort involving the state, the communities, and the housing co-operatives. The last policy points directly to the issue of complexity.

The plan indicates a series of concrete initiatives: expellation of resource-weak and misadjusted inhabitants; to make the area more attractive to resource-strong applicants; to allow the community to give lower priority to immigrants and resource-weak applicants and higher priority to resource-strong applicants; to allow the community to overrule the housing co-operative councils; to allow to reduce social benefits in order to admonish deviance and strengthen control of social fraud; to increase punishment of violence or hindrance of public duties; to offer day schools for adults, flexible school districts, job centres and local work practices; to initiative co-operation between police, communities and housing co-operatives via local councils and to issue a note on partnership with Muslim groups. This list is mentioned here in detail, in order to stress that none of its actual initiatives are related to the assigned core issue concerning values. Whereas ghettoization is regarded as a complex problem, it is approached in practice as a set of separate issues which can be handled by more control and a little more incentive for work. Complexity is addressed in relation to pointing out a need for co-operation between the police, the community and the housing co-operatives, but the plan does not indicate how it can be established.

It is noteworthy that the preamble of the plan points out values as the core issue. However, the plan does not contain any initiatives for disseminating values among the ghettoized population. It rather purges those inhabitants who seem to deviate from the proclaimed values. It is an open question where those purged from the ghettoes shall find a new home.

This plan was countered by a joint initiative proposed by the major opposition parties, Socialdemokratiet and Socialistisk Folkeparti. This plan focused on insecurity and anxiety as the core of the problem, but it also mentioned the ethnic composition of the community as an aspect of the problem. The plan consisted of three 'phases': 1. 'A firm hand' which involved a new force of 220 'ghetto police officers', and a 'fast track' for young offenders, zones of prohibition, and social welfare sanctions. 2. A changed composition of the inhabitants. This involved to build social housing which could receive inhabitants who move out from the ghettos, and to attract newcomers and workplaces by lower rents. 3. Investment in housing and people. This part of the plan involved making the housing more attractive and introduced social regulations, such as a ceiling on the proportion of pupils who do not have Danish as their primary language, demands that family-based immigrants seek jobs, and initiatives for better job training.

This plan has many similarities with the government's. However, it addresses safety rather than values as the core issue. It does not analyze which conditions in the ghettos which produce unsafety. The relation between the issue of safety and the proposed initiatives is not made explicit. The main mechanism of the proposal is also here social sanctions. The inhabitants seem to be regarded as part of the problem rather as partners for its solution. This is somewhat odd, as unsafety is mainly an internal problem, whereas the creation of a parallel society is mainly an external problem.

Both ghetto plans rest on assumptions which have not been documented. The Liberal-Conservative plan assumes that the formation of ghettos is voluntary, and that the ghettos are breeding grounds for a specific set of values which differ from those prevalent in Danish society. This amounts to an assumption about voluntary separation. This assumption corresponds with the general agenda of the Liberal-Conservative government of a struggle for 'the Danish values', which are especially threatened by Islamic values. The plan attempts to break up a tight clique of people who obstinately pursues its specific culture and values. This corresponds with an image of the social ghettos as Muslim townships within Denmark. Whereas the plan refers to indicators of multi-ethnicity, there is no documentation of the ethnic homogeneity among the residents. A community may have a large proportion of residents with an immigrant background, but this does not indicate that they are Muslims, or that their beliefs lead them to support values which are in contrast to the ones ascribed to Danish society by the government.

The voluntaristic assumption can be questioned by regarding simulations of residence patterns (Epstein & Axtell 1996). Already a generation ago, Schelling demonstrated that a separation of residencies does not have to result from any wish to split the community. Even a weak preference to have neighbours who are similar to oneself may result in a separation. The voluntaristic assumption is especially problematic regarding those inhabitants with few resources. Their range of options on the house market is very restricted, and as newcomers they have little knowledge about their options and consequences of their choice. It is more probable that a voluntary separation results from exclusion among those who have access to ample resources. They have the option to buy a house in a neighbourhood with few immigrants and few social clients.

In a similar manner, the opposition plan assumes that the social ghettos are subject to an illegal internal power structure. The plan addresses a kind of fear which can be addressed to a specific mafia or gang. However, there is not any documentation that organized crime is prevalent in the social ghettos. While it may be correct that unsafety is a major issue, it may rest on an entirely different situation. An anomic anguish is prevalent in situations where people feel disoriented; where there are no shared norms for what is right and wrong in everyday life, and where people cannot predict what others do or trust their neighbours implicitly. While a structured fear has a target. Anomic anguish is devoid of such a target (Durkheim 1964, Berger 1972). However, an anomic anguish may lead to establish such a target by appointing scape-goats.

A plan which rests on false assumptions may result in unanticipated, negative consequences. Thus, political efforts to counter islamistic values may end with a dissolution of all values; and efforts to motivate more mobility may end with people becoming more uprooted and less integrated in Danish society. Efforts to counter the fear from gangs may lead to more anomic anguish.

4. Social Ghettos as Sociotopes

'Ghetto' is a misleading term. Those communities which have been singled out by the Liberal-Conservative government as ghettos have little in common with the insulated quarters where Jews were obliged to live. Many of those communities designated as ghettos are actually modern and comfortable with green areas. Their ethnic composition is heterogeneous. However, the economic standard of the inhabitants is generally below the average. There are many inhabitants on low-income jobs, on pensions or social support. The so-called ghettos can be regarded as sociotopes: a community with a specific socio-economic composition of the inhabitants, characterized by internal and external processes of inclusion and exclusion.

Society is composed of many sociotopes, which vary in their degree of homogeneity and insulation. One of the more conspicuous sociotopes is the one north of Copenhagen where the economic elite lives in relative seclusion. There are local connections between the formation of sociotopes. The sociotope for the economic elite is mirrored in the 'ghettoized' sociotopes. When a certain segment of society is concentrated in one sociotope, it is logically absent in others. The comfort of the affluent sociotope is assured by establishing sociotopes for their unwanted neighbours. A policy of dissolving social ghettos implies to move the people to other communities. It is not likely that any will be moved from the social ghettos to the affluent sociotopes. They are more likely to move to other low-income communities, and it is not assured that these people will be welcomed. This migration may even lead to new tensions and end with new social ghettos.

Public sanctioning is not the best approach to social integration, neither internally nor with society at large. The network of neighbours is probably a better instrument for strengthening the internal norms. One possible outcome of the ghetto policies is that the internal networks become dissolved due to migration and external sanctions. An increased migration may dissolve fragile networks. Relatively well-integrated inhabitants may look askew to neighbours who are on social benefits, who do not speak Danish well, or who have a criminal record. Instead of supporting mutual support and internal solidarity, the ghetto plans may lead to an internal fragmentation and exclusion. In order to avoid a general stigmatization of the whole community an internal stigmatization of the misfits may take place. Both ghetto plans point to trust and safety as basic values, but they may increase distrust and internal conflicts.

The public institution for research on housing, Statens Byggeforskningsinstitut, presented a report on life in a social ghetto: "Om at bo i et multietnisk område" (Hansen et al. 2009). The report focused on the multi-ethnic composition of the community. It was based on qualitative interviews with about 150 inhabitants and about 30 professionals who somehow provided public services for a multi-ethnic community. The study covered three neighbourhoods who fullfilled the government's criteria for a social ghetto.

The problems of such neighbourhoods look quite different seen from the outside and seen from the inside. The report stressed two problems which were stressed by the inhabitants. Firstly, some few households were noisy and messy. It was quite easy for other inhabitants to point out the few trouble-makers. The problems were solved internally in some cases, while the administration or the police had to be involved in others. Both immigrants and native Danes were involved in the troublemaking households. The report does not provide information about the background of these households. If these households are composed of traumatized refugees or un-social Danes, then the source of the problems cannot be traced to the community as such. People with such a background may trigger problems wherever they live. The very density of the neighbourhood amplifies the troubles. However, in order to solve the foundation of the problems, therapy and social work is called for rather than public sanctions.

The second problem mentioned by the inhabitants consisted of youngsters who threaten and harass other inhabitants. The report tells about an insecurity which corresponds with the main issue of the opposition's ghetto plan. However, the report indicates that this fear is not so much based on personal experiences. It is more based on gossip among neighbours and from the press. There is a general worry about forming gangs and that their own children can be attracted by a gang. It is stressed by the report that actual gangs include a minority of the young inhabitants. According to the report, the core group of young trouble-makers is relatively easy to identify. The majority of young people in the community behave normally according to the Danish norms for young people, which are quite liberal.

A point which the report does not make explicit but which we may infer is a latent tension between two sections of the population. Some of the inhabitants in the community are retired Danes, who feel uncomfortable with the young generation of immigrants. There is a gap between these fractions which is due to differences in generation, culture, and norms. The elderly may feel the kind of insecurity stressed by the oppositions' plan. However, it is questionable whether the proposed policy represents the best solution. A 'ghetto-police' and 'fast-track'-sanctions can only be operative at decisively criminal actions. The worries are rather directed to minor harassments, where regulations from the neighbourhood are called for. Interestingly enough, some police directors participated in the public debate and noticed that the ghetto problems were social problems rather than criminal problems.

The studied communities are not ghettos in the sense that an immigrant group predominates them. They are multi-ethnic in a radical sense. There is a general wish among the inhabitants to have more Danish neighbours in the community, because this could help integration into the larger Danish society. Contacts between neighbours are mostly sporadic and superficial. Many talk about mutual assistance among neighbours but few have close contact with other residents. Really close friends are relatives or friends with a similar ethnic background who in most cases live in another neighbourhood. The report hints that many of the inhabitants are relatively isolated within the community and in Danish society at large. Contacts with other neighbours are described as polite but spontaneous and superficial. Danes are regarded by residents with an immigrant background as quite polite but also as reserved, cold and distant. The community is not seen as based on residential democracy of which they are an active part. Some even think that there is a private owner. The administration is encountered as a distant bureaucracy which sends out bills and incomprehensible letters.

The report stresses language problems as a barrier to the kind of contact between neighbours which can build solidary actions in order to protect against the encountered problems. While the ghetto plans include initiatives to improve the Danish language, these seem directed more towards the children than among the adults. One aspect of the complex problem seems to be that several of the inhabitants are not able to relate to a rationalized, impersonal bureaucracy. This problem is shared by both immigrants and ethnic Danes with a basic schooling. It is not just related to understanding Danish but to understanding the type communication used by the public authorities. In order to overcome a sense of alienation from and distrust against Danish bureaucracy, it would probably be more efficient to send out a staff of advisors who could help inhabitants to present their actual problems to the proper offices. The opposition's plan involves a ghetto police force. Maybe it would improve its credibility if it were simultaneously to assist inhabitants at their contact with the public authorities, including addressing their rights to protest against decisions from public authorities.

5. Sociology's contribution to studying social ghettos

The problem is not that we lack information about the social ghettos. There is a lot of statistical information available. There are many reports from architects, engineers, economists. There are also studies about social life. Some further sociological studies could maybe contribute to the general knowledge. However, what is basically needed is not a series of particular sociological studies of some selected aspects of the social composition of the inhabitants or their social life.

What is mostly needed is an approach which may bring the scattered pieces of information together. This challenge is not particular for sociologists. All university students are admonished to focus and narrow down a problem to a manageable research question. Otherwise, their study would probably result in a diffuse, abstract and vague essay. However, by stressing the analytical aspect of research, the synthetic one is too often ignored. The predominance of analysis over synthesis is also reflected in textbooks on sociological methods. They typically propose either quantitative or qualitative research designs as two entirely different types. Sociology as a discipline depends on both quantitative and qualitative information, both extensive and intensive studies. Therefore, discussions on methodology have increasing abandoned this divide and taken up considerations about mixed methods (Bryman 1988, Tashakkori and Teddlie 1998, Riis 2001). One important step towards obtaining an integrated knowledge is taken by combining qualitative and quantitative information. With a complex problem, such as social ghettos, there is an obvious need for combining both types of information. It is relevant to obtain knowledge about populations' demographic composition and cultural characteristisc; about its economic status and its quality of life; about crime rates and its social norms; about educational statistics and school experiences. Encounters with real social problems rather than desktop problems direct sociologists to consider mixing methods. However, the challenge of methodological integration is even more complex. It involves, for instance, to combine phenomenological perceptions with cognitive interpretations; or to combine structural information about the community with personal information about how individual agents relate to it. Furthermore, sociologists need to consider how the information they produce about the community as a social field may be combined with other types of information, which are relevant for improving life in it.

All the specialists involved contribute to these discussions in their own professional language, and they often misunderstand each other. Sociologists therefore need to consider how they may contribute fruitfully. While each academic discipline is focused on developing its own theories in order to obtain consistency in the internal discourses, there is less attention to the need for communicating with other specialists. This also holds for sociologists, despite our claim to take an overarching view on social life. Despite the obvious need, few resources are invested in the elaboration of a meta-language which may enable us to translate and relate the specialized languages. In practice, some kind of meta-language is developed when the specialists meet representatives for the inhabitants and discuss their problems. It is my impression that architects are the most skilled in forming a meta-language ad hoc which allows communication between the specialists and with the inhabitants.

Sociologists could also contribute, not only with their specialist knowledge, but to forming a meta-language which can express the social aspects of the complex. However, to develop such a meta-language is a special challenge. Sociological theories generally consist of either very abstract 'grand theories' or specific but narrowly focused 'particular theories'. While it is difficult to relate the concrete information to the grand theories, it is also difficult to connect information gathered by different particularistic theories. By addressing such a problem as social ghettos, it becomes evident that there is a need for sociology to consider how its subdisciplines may be joined. Thus, information about the demography of a community needs to be connected with information about family patterns and family life, and further with information about the foundation of family ideals in culture and religion. There is no need for another 'grand theory' as the type described by C.W. Mills 1970. But there is a dire need for a conceptual framework which allows sociologists to connect the particular pieces of information.

Sociological theories can form a part of that framework, but they can hardly cover all aspects of the complex. Some sociological theories have a high level of generality, but they are very abstract, and it is difficult to relate the relevant empirical information to them. Some sociological theories are directly relevant for issues relating to the studies of social ghettos. But these theories tend to be particularistic, ignoring other equally relevant issues. It is therefore hard to use the prevailing theories as a framework for connecting all the relevant sociological issues. Furthermore, these partial sociological theories seldom address connections to other types of issues. Nevertheless, sociologists can bring their experiences with constructions of theories into the shared task by forming a meta-framework for discussing how the complex can be approached as a set of dimensions, which can be illuminated by a multi-disciplinary approach, including sociology.

As for many other academic disciplines, sociology is characterized by internal debates about paradigms. By confronting complex problems, the parochialism of these debates is revealed. Each paradigm represents a certain view of the role of sociology and its performance. This may help to clarify what sociology may provide to an interdisciplinary team. However, in order to collaborate in an interdisciplinary team work, sociology has to to be open-minded, internally and externally. Studies of complex social problems call for many types of knowledge, and must therefore rely on a combination of methods. Sociologists need to study official documents, statistics, perform field observations and biographic interviews. Furthermore, sociologists have to collaborate with other specialists which rely on other epistemologies and methods.

6. Complications and Complexity

Epistemology is basically an ongoing debate about how to obtain knowledge which we can rely on. It does not form fixed dogmatic positions which we must adhere to. Methodology is basically a reflection on how to produce that kind of knowledge. It does not determine ritualistically fixed actions which need to be performed in the name of science. An interdisciplinary approach to complex problems calls for an open mind, although not for a relativism which increases the sense of confusion.

Some problems are experienced as chaotically complicated in the sense that they are incomprehensible and the outcome is unpredictable. A chaotic complication seems insolvable and therefore leads to passivity or flight. It involves an active stance to address a problem as complex. It is a challenge to comprehend and predict the processes involved in the problem, but it is not impossible. A complex social problem refers to an open system of related processes.

To address a problem as complex implies a claim that it is possible to structure the problem in a systematic manner which makes the outcome of interventions more predictable. The type of complex problems referred to above involve human beings, who do not just react to stimuli in a mechanical manner. Human beings interpret the situation, they are situated in, and act according to their interpretation and expectation. The human aspect does not make open systems volatile and unpredictable. Our daily life is performed in an open system, which we are able to interpret successfully. With the inclusion of the human aspect in considerations about complexity, a hermeneutical stance is called for. This stance is pronounced in some branches of the social sciences, including sociology, while it is bracketed by the natural and technical sciences.

Complex problems have a multidimensional character which calls for a constellation of several types of knowledge, about economic, legal, statistical, technical, architectural, pedagogical, psychological, cultural – and sociological aspects. The problem is recognized as being beyond the agenda of a singular field of expertise. It necessitates a constellation and exchange between several fields of knowledge. It contains an epistemic challenge to trained academics, including sociologists. It not only involves different fields of knowledge, but also different layers of conditions and different aspects of causality. Some disciplines address causal mechanisms, some conditions for change, and some intentions and motives for change; some focus on empirical regularities whereas others refer to latent potentials for change. All these aspects are relevant in order to facilitate processes which may ameliorate the problem. Furthermore, complex social problems typically involve causal sequences. Some types of processes depend on certain conditions to have an impact. Some of these processual relations are hierarchical, in the sense that dependence is one-sided, and some are dialectical, in the sense that the processes feed back on each other. One of the major tasks of addressing complexity is to identify the types of relations between the types of processes identified.

To address complexity implies to differentiate a set of related dimensions. This differentiation involves some degree of reduction, where aspects are bracketed, since they do not seem to have a predictable effect on the series of processes. An analytical reduction does not imply a simplification of the problem, where the complication is solved by reduction to one basic dimension. Some problems can be simplified in this manner, because the complication is due to approaching the problem from an erroneous angle. However, many social problems are complex, as they involve several interrelated types of processes, and to address them by a simplification leads to unanticipated consequences, which increase to sense of complication even more.

Each academic discipline has developed an internal paradigm, a language and methodology, which enables it to focus on a specific type of problems and produce relevant and valid knowledge about it. Each disciplinary paradigm rests on a specified set of assumptions, and the theoretical language is derived from these with logical consistency. However, this does not imply that the theories are incompatible or untranslatable. In our daily life, we routinely shift between perspectives and combine many types of knowledge. We even recognize that it is problematic to stick to just one perspective in a complex situation. An interdisciplinary dialogue represents an elaboration of the epistemic combinations of everyday life. The shared resource for mutual understanding is the shift of perspectives in our daily life.

A complex approach differs from simplification on the one hand and holism on the other. Simplification implies that the problem is reduced to one basic factor, while holism attempts to include all possible factors in the analysis. While simplification involves a reduction to one concrete factor, holism involves a reduction to one abstract entity. Postulates about holism are basically metaphysical and cannot be subject to rational discourse. Referring to the problem discussed above, social ghettos can be approached either by simplification or holism. Some regard its complication as illusory as they ascribe the problem to one issue, such as the technical standard or the appointment of flats. Some regard the complications as derived from one overarching issue, such as social values, fear, or economic deprivation. A complex approach is different from these by addressing the problem as involving several types of interrelated processes. In practice, this leads to an approach which operates with several types of incentives and mechanisms simultaneously.

Several disciplines are involved in a complex approach, and none of these can claim primacy. Each discipline provides analyses of its special dimensions. In order to form a synthesis, these dimensions need to be related to each other. One suitable metaphor is to weave a basket in a spontaneous teamwork without a pre-existing model. Interdisciplinary discourses indicate possible connections which must be tried out in practice. Some connections prove to be fragile while others point to potential solutions. The synthesis grows from practice and it is by practicing it that it may be evaluated.

The synthetic challenge is especially marked in the encounter between the natural sciences and the humanities. The advance of positivistic natural science and the answer from Neo-Kantianism created a communicative gap. Natural sciences, humanities and social sciences represent different academic discourses which vary regarding their research objects and their understanding of scientific 'truth'. While the purely academic discourses seem very diverse, practitioners are often able to combine these perspectives effectively. Practicing medical doctors routinely combine approaches from the natural sciences with social and humanistic ones. A similar combination can be found among architects, who both address technical, social and aesthetic challenges. However, academic discourses on epistemology and methodology seldom reflect on such practical manners of combining knowledge.

Considerations about social complex problems thereby lead to some kind of pragmatism. Pragmatism can be a profound reflection on how knowledge can be evaluated by our human application of it. Sociology has a well-established school of pragmatism, which originated with the Fabians at London School of Economics and the Chicago school in USA. Several of the prominent contemporary sociologists affiliate themselves with some kind of pragmatism, including Pierre Bourdieu, Jürgen Habermas and Hans Joas. However, this kind of pragmatism contains a critical dimension, which goes beyond simple utilitarian purposes such as profit or power. One of the challenges of a critical pragmatic approach is to determine the complex aim which answers the complex problem. Referring to the example of the social ghettos, a complex goal would involve considerations about the life quality of the inhabitants and the long-term benefits for society at large.

When politicians or financiers launch complex problems, they often assume a simplified, utilitarian agenda. Academic disciplines become involved indirectly through its practitioners. It is a basic challenge to establish a basic resistance against being subject to a narrow, short-sighted utilitarian agenda. Some academics react by retracting to a pristine insulation. However, it is more fruitful to encounter reductionism and utilitarianism by accepting the challenge of complexity and to prepare for engaging with such problems in a pragmatic albeit critical manner. This also involves openness to collaboration with other disciplines. The academic society is inherently fragmented and therefore victim to a policy of divide and rule. However, by addressing the issue of complexity it may form a unified front in public debates which opposes simplifications, such as those which disregard the human, social and aesthetic aspects of social ghettos.

References

Bell, Daniel 1976, *The Coming of Post-Industrial Society*, New York: Basic Books.

Berger, Peter L. 1972, *Den samfundsskabte virkelighed*, København: Lindhardt og Ringhof, Alma.

Bryman, Alan 1988, *Quantity and Quality in Social Research,* London: Routledge.

Durkheim, Émile 1964, *The division of labour in society*, New York: The Free Press. Macmillan.

Epstein, Joshua M. and Axtell, Robert 1996, *Growing Artificial Societies. Social Science from the Bottom Up*, Washington D.C.: Brookings Institute Press. Cambridge: The MIT Press.

Gundelach, Peter and Riis, Ole 1992, *Danskernes Værdier*, København: Forlaget Sociologi.

Hansen, Knud Erik et al. 2009. Om at bo i et multietnisk boligområde. SBI 2010:01. Aalborg.

Mills, C. Wright 1970, *The Sociological Imagination*, Harmondsworth: Penguin Books.

Møller, Ib et al. 1981. *Byfornyelse – det drejer sig om mennesker*, Beder: Møller & Grønborg.

Møller, Ib et al. 1981, *Skitse til Christiania-områdets fremtidige anvendelse*, Beder: Møller & Grønborg.

Oppositionens ghettoplan:
http://sfu.dk/news/s-sf-freml%C3%A6gger-ghettoplan/.

Rambøll, JyllandsPosten 2010:
http://jp.dk/indland/article2254165.ece.

Regeringens ghettoplan:
http://www.b.dk/danmark/her-er-regeringens-32 ghettointiativer.
http://www.sm.dk/Nyheder/Sider/Vis%20Nyhed.aspx?NewsItem=526.

Riis, Ole 2001, *Metoder på tværs. Om forudsætningen for sociologisk metodekombination*, København: Jurist- og Økonomforbundets Forlag.

Tashakkori, Abbas and Charles Teddlie, 1998, *Mixed methodology. Combining Qualitative and Quantitative Approaches,* London: Sage Publications.

Michael Springer

Physical Complexity

1. Simplify your life!

At first sight, the world is bewildering.

Recently, a friend of mine lost his cognitive abilities almost completely from one moment to the next. Speechless, he looked around like a space traveller in a science-fiction novel who has suddenly been beamed to some strange planet, or like a toddler in a pram who stares at the large heads of grinning grown-ups approaching dangerously close.

My friend suffered from Herpesviral encephalitis. For months, he lost most of memory and speech. Now, after he has almost completely recovered, he speaks of that time as a complete blank, a dreamless sleep from which he suddenly awoke. Apparently, during his illness he lived only in the Here-and-Now, without past or future. His cognitive abilities appeared to be less than those of higher animals. When a meal was put before him, he seemingly pondered what to do with it; for some time, he had to be fed. Only his reflexes worked: He opened his mouth for the approaching spoon, and he swallowed the food in his mouth.

In "Der logische Aufbau der Welt" the logical positivist Rudolf Carnap in 1928 tried to build the world from scratch, i.e. from "Elementarerlebnissen" (elementary experiences, "atomic" phenomena of consciousness) and one single "Ähnlichkeitsrelation" (similarity relation). My friend, when ill, was certainly not able to build a world in this way; his memory did not work properly, and so no coherent similarities between his experiences could be firmly established.

In one sense, the encephalitis radically simplified my friend's life, reducing it to elementary facts without structure, i.e. without any amount of complexity. Maybe his experience at least comprised some short-lived separate "things" like spoons, strange people or drinkable fluids – which à la Carnap would take quite some work to constitute out of elementary similarities of sense data – but those objects were not hierarchically structured. Rather than constituting his world as a complex multi-storey building, they lay around like so many bricks on an infinite plane.

Because of its lack of complexity, this private world was very simple. But in a practical sense, the lack of similarity-constituting memory complicated my friend's life immensely. Left alone, he would have died. He needed help: the complicated intentional actions of physicians, nurses and friends had to compensate for the non-complexity of his structurally "flat" world.

By the way, this situation corresponds to that of a Buddhist who has achieved complete enlightenment. He would regard all facts of life as equally (un)important, would do no work and could survive only as long as other people supplied him with clothing and nourishment.

2. Complex models reduce complex facts

For all practical purposes and contrary to what the word implies: Complexity makes things easier. We need this concept to organise and simplify our practical knowledge. In most instances it would be unnecessary – and only disorienting – to keep track of all the elementary aspects of the things we handle. We structure our experience by constructing models as simple as possible and as complex as necessary, and as we try to apply them, we know all the time: any model, as complex as it may be, is less complicated than the reality it tries to render – probably infinitely less so.

We might articulate this state of affairs as the statement: "Reality is infinitely complex." In fact this seemingly metaphysical statement makes perfect sense. It just means, first, that any practicable model must be less complex than the things it models, because otherwise it would be of no practical use; and, second, that nobody knows in advance if and when this modelling will ever come to an end. So any complex model reduces complexity, and therefore its complexity makes things simpler and life easier.

3. An elementary example from physics

In astonishingly recent times, physicists still debated if atoms existed at all. Austrian philosopher-physicist Ernst Mach (1838-1916) was a firm positivist and sensualist. He believed only in empirically confirmed sense-data and regarded any statement about things residing in an objective reality as pure metaphysics, i. e. nonsense. Since at his time nobody could imagine a microscope that would make single atoms visible, he invariably got furious if anybody mentioned atoms and used to snigger: "Ham's eins g'sehn?" (Ever seen one?).

Mach's main adversary was another Austrian physicist, Ludwig Boltzmann (1844-1906), a firm atomist. He – and the Scottish physicist James Clerk Maxwell (1831-1879) – developed statistical thermodynamics, a theory of heat based on the movement of atoms.

As mentioned, it was then impossible to observe single atoms, even less to measure their individual locations and velocities. Today we could achieve that in principle – but even small macroscopic bodies or amounts of gases contain so many atoms that even modern supercomputers cannot track them all. However, it is not necessary to observe every single microscopic particle in order to describe how the macroscopic object they constitute behaves. If water is put on a stove, the water molecules move faster and faster, and the fastest of them escape as vapour. In everyday life we – as well as experimental physicists in Mach's and Boltzmann's time – do not bother to observe single water particles; we just measure by thermometer that the water gets warmer, and we can watch how it partly evaporates and finally boils at 100 degrees Celsius.

In their theory of thermodynamics, Maxwell and Boltzmann, so to say, took advantage of our lack of knowledge about the fate of each and every atom in a gas, by applying statistics to large ensembles of particles. What does Temperature mean? It is a measure of the average kinetic energy of particles: the higher the average energy, the hotter the gas, and vice versa. What is Pressure? It is the force of the particles (per square unit) hitting the wall of the gas container with average kinetic energy. So, the macroscopic state of a system (characterized by volume, temperature, pressure) emerges from its microscopic state (ideally described by the locations and velocities of every particle) by describing the latter statistically.

And what is Entropy, the most intriguing concept of thermodynamics? In the theory of heat, first developed to describe steam-engines, the power-horses of the Industrial Revolution, entropy had been introduced as a measure of the dissipation of thermal energy: If we use heat to drive a motor, some of the thermal energy is always lost into the environment. Entropy increases.

Now Boltzmann defined entropy in terms of atoms: as the logarithm of the sum of all the microscopic states of a system that yield the same macroscopic state. Entropy thus tells us how many different configurations of all the system's tiny particles can be regarded as macroscopically equal, as corresponding to one and the same state of the system as a whole. For example, it would make no difference if we exchanged two particles in the gas and let each behave as the other one. Generally speaking, we could modify the locations and velocities of some particles in many subtle ways that would not influence the overall picture. The (logarithm of the) sum of all those microscopic possibilities yields the entropy of the big system. (The logarithm in the brackets has technical reasons).

This abstract definition of entropy is often illustrated by "disorder": the growth of entropy is equivalent to growing disorder. For example, a homogenously distributed gas filling a volume in thermal equilibrium can have many more microscopically equivalent states than the same gas inhomogenously concentrated in one corner of the same volume or having a velocity distribution far from equilibrium. In the former case entropy and "disorder" are high, in the latter case both are low.

4. Emergence

As I casually stated above, the macroscopic state of a system "emerges" from its microscopic state. As far as the macroscopic quantities volume, pressure and temperature are concerned, their emergence seems rather primitive: A vast number of micro-quantities are statistically compressed into three macro-quantities. In this case, emergence just reduces the complexity of the behaviour of many atoms by characterising their average behaviour – but isn't that a disappointing transformation? Emergence, as it is generally understood, should not only simplify complex phenomena, but also create something new; from a complex system, it should produce "more than the sum of its parts", not less!

In favour of the "emergent" quantities volume V, temperature T and pressure p one could at least argue that they satisfy the macroscopic equation of state for ideal gases $p \cdot V = const \cdot T$, which can be readily deduced from the hit-and-run movement of microscopic point-like gas particles using the above-mentioned statistical interpretation of those quantities. But the real magic of emergence is indeed performed by entropy. As is well known, this macro-quantity is not only connected with the disorder of a state, but also with the probability of that state. In any system left to its own resources, disorder is more probable than order, so closed systems will naturally develop towards disorder and higher entropy.

Now, this direction of development (stated in the Second Law of Thermodynamics, which postulates that the entropy of closed systems never decreases) really creates something new: It introduces the arrow of time into physics. The fact that past and future are not the same, indeed "emerges" from the statistical description of complex microsystems.

This is really something! The progress of time emerges from statistics! When Boltzmann formulated his theory, colleagues shook their heads. They argued: All basic laws of physics remain unchanged if the direction of time is reversed. The orbits of planets, the curve of a thrown stone, the collision of billiard balls – all that can develop the other way round in time without violating any law of physics. All the microphysical interactions of gas particles, idealized as tiny billiard balls, are reversible; but as a statistical ensemble, they really behave irreversibly!

So by radically simplifying the complex interactions of myriads of particles through a statistical description, our macro-world, irreversibly developing from past to future, emerges from a completely reversible micro-world. Generalizing this fundamental example, we may now define Emergence as the creation of a qualitatively new property through the reduction of complexity.

As the example illustrates, the emergent property lies nearer to our everyday experience than the system out of which it emerges. Our lives happen in time; we remember the past and do not know what the future may hold. Before our eyes, completely reversible processes never really happen; they are abstractions, idealizations. Philosophically speaking – using a remark by Karl Marx in his "Einleitung zur Kritik der Politischen Ökonomie" concerning the progress of knowledge about the complex systems of economy – we might say: Emergence ascends from the abstract to the concrete.

5. How real is emergence?

What could be more real than a "concrete" fact of everyday experience, like time's arrow? However, since emergent properties appear through the reduction of complex systems, one might argue that only those complex systems are real, whereas emergence is not. This would be the radical reductionist view. In fact, theoretical physicists who deal with Einstein's general relativity and who try – for the time being without success – to integrate it with quantum mechanics into a Theory of Everything called quantum gravity, tend to regard time simply as the fourth coordinate of spacetime; they describe the world as a four-dimensional "block universe" which is just there. What we experience as development would be just that which happens if we move along the time coordinate; in reality as a whole, everything would be fixed forever. In this sense, Einstein regarded time as an illusion.

Paradoxically, we tend to regard a fact of life the more as an "illusion", the better this fact is understood, i.e. the more it can be explained as emergent. Such has been the case with mental phenomena just recently; of course, the basis for a reductionist view of mental phenomena is the advance of brain research and neuroscience. If in the famous experiments by Benjamin Libet a person decides to move a finger at a certain moment and if during the decision process her brain activity is exactly monitored in time, the decision process is reduced to neurophysiological interactions – and our "free will" seems to be exposed as an illusion. (Libet found that the brain becomes active even before the proband's decision, but this dubious result only exacerbated the general effect of this kind of experiment.)

Regarding emergence, it is not easy to stay on course between the Scylla of "essentialism" (ontological multiplicity) and the Charybdis of "illusionism" (radical reductionism). First, let's avoid omnivorous Charybdis, which is not difficult, since it just concerns a manner of speaking: Obviously, there is no need to throw any concept overboard as "mere illusion" just because it can be explained scientifically – which always means reduced to something else. We continue to speak of temperature, although we know it is "merely" the random movement of atoms; we describe and analyze thoughts and other mental phenomena, although they are "merely" neural interactions; we appreciate songs about sunrise and sunset, although we have known for centuries that the movement of the sun is "merely" an illusion caused by the rotation of the earth.

On the other hand there looms the ancient "essentialistic" monster Scylla, proudly presenting its multiple ontological bodies. However, its deadly enemy is science, armed with Occam's razor. Any fact of life that has been scientifically explained, i.e. reduced, instantly loses its essential quality of being-what-it-is, of a fact that needs no explanation. For example, "free will" used to be an intuitively compelling (although philosophically contentious) concept – a causeless cause for spontaneous action. By describing the physiological background of decision-making, science "deconstructs" any essentialist concept of absolute freedom. In this sense, "free will" certainly turns out to be an illusion. But that does not imply that we are not accountable for our actions. The statement that whatever we decide and do is the outcome of microscopic (atomic, chemical, physiological) processes rightly circumscribes the realm of science, but otherwise it is empty, impractical – downright metaphysical. It explains nothing about how I would behave in a typical moral dilemma, in which I (the "I" is an emergent quality) have to decide (intentions and decisions are emergent) between right and wrong or "good" and "bad" (highly emergent alternatives).

Concerning another instance of essentialist error, it is intuitively appealing to regard oneself and others as physical bodies inhabited and steered by invisible spiritual minds. Children spontaneously develop this "theory of mind", and most cultures and religions adhere to modified versions of it. Again, this dualistic essentialism has been gradually expelled by science and is now exposed as an illusion – although we will certainly continue to regard mental phenomena as different from bodily processes like digestion.

As has "metaphysically" been stated above, reality is complex, even infinitely so. But that does not necessarily imply that any reduction of complexity must be less real. A reduction can be more or less adequate. We recognize a successful reduction by the fact that it adequately reproduces some traditional, perhaps even pre-scientific concept, which may have been in use since ancient times, but was never before recognised as an emergent quality. In this process, the traditional concept is explicated – explained, reduced and modified. Often such a re-interpretation is not readily accepted; it may take decades or even centuries to establish it, as is the way with cultural changes.

We may regard such an adequate, successful reduction of complexity as indicating a "real" case of emergence. If a description of an abstract complex system via complexity-reduction leads to emergent concrete properties that we knew beforehand but regarded as belonging to the unexplainable facts of life, then we have detected true emergence.

6. What Complexity cannot achieve

Since Complexity and Emergence are very general concepts, they have a seductive appeal; they seem to contain the promise for a unified theory of structures and their development. However, in themselves those concepts have no explanatory power; they just denote instances of "qualitative" change, like the phase transition of fluid water to gas at its boiling point.

In fact, notions connected to complexity have not kept their promise of supplying the basis for a general theory of nature. In the 1980s many papers had "chaos" and "fractal" in their title, and the Belgian Nobel laureate Ilya Prigogine (1917-2003) proclaimed a change of scientific methodology "from Being to Becoming". He had analyzed chemical processes far from thermal equilibrium and found diverse instances of spontaneous development of ordered structures. In his later years, he tried to create a general theory of self-organisation, including ant societies and human settlements.

The French-American mathematician Benoit Mandelbrot (1924-2010), working as a researcher for IBM, 1975 published a ground-breaking book about the "fractal geometry of nature". In the 1980s personal computers became common goods, and they could now produce fascinating pictures of journeys through the infinite "self-similar" details of the famous Mandelbrot set. Fractal sets seemed to supply the appropriate mathematics for the description of "rough" or "chaotic" phenomena, from coastlines and cauliflowers to stock markets.

The technical basis of these developments was the general availability of computers; they can simulate the behaviour of "chaotic" nonlinear systems and can numerically calculate recursive functions with great speed. Nowadays supercomputers provide reliable weather forecasts and comprehensive climate models, simulate "chaotic" combustion processes or calculate complex interactions of fundamental particles.

Those are great achievements, but they did not pave the way to a unified theory of complex phenomena. In fact, Priogogine in the end even tried to develop a fundamental theory of quantum mechanics based on mathematical concepts from statistical thermodynamics, including time's arrow – but he did not succeed.

From this failure, a general lesson might be learned. The evolution of complex systems can, by emergence, create hierarchies of phenomena, corresponding to domains of science, one resting on the other like the storeys of a tower. This evolution, as described by John Maynard Smith and Eörs Szathmáry 1995 in "The Major Transitions in Evolution", leads "upwards" to ever more complex models: from elementary physics to statistical ensembles and chemistry, from those to biochemistry and biology and further on to the study of ecology and societies. But emergence is a one-way ticket; the explanatory escalator in this hierarchical building goes only up, not down. It is possible to explain the next-higher level by deriving its complex phenomena from the greater complexity of the lower one, but not the other way round. The fundamental physics of quantum mechanics cannot be described with the mathematical tools of the next level, of thermodynamics. The arrow of time ("Becoming") belongs to the higher level, to statistical theory; it cannot be projected downward into the basic level of reversible particle physics, to the realm of "Being".

A similar mistake seems to be made by some physicists who have tried to introduce the concept of "information" as the basis for an interpretation of quantum physics. They conclude that physical reality, on its most fundamental quantum level, consists neither of matter nor energy, but of information. However, like entropy, any quantifiable concept of information does belong to the next-higher level, to statistical thermodynamics, rather than to time-symmetric quantum mechanics.

Still less can highly emergent mental phenomena like intentions, decisions or "free will" be somehow directly deduced from the basic uncertainty principle of quantum mechanics, although this recurring idea seems to have perennial appeal. Quantum mechanical uncertainty must not be interpreted as some basic freedom of decision.

This example shows: Even when emergence seems to work in the "right", i.e. "upward" direction, it can go wrong, if there happens an instance of "Sphärenvermengung" (mixture of domains), to use an expression coined by Carnap. A well-known example is Social Darwinism. It applies biological concepts like "struggle for life" and "survival of the fittest" to sociology; in this way, the metaphorical expressions Darwin coined for his explanation of biological evolution – in fact inspired by contemporary Malthusian ideas about society – are misunderstood as "scientifically derived" aims and values for human culture. However, between biological populations and human societies there emerges a specific difference not to be ignored: The fundamental principle underlying biological evolution is genetic heredity; human populations and their histories develop by cultural inheritance.

On the other hand, their emergent difference does not imply that the two domains have absolutely nothing in common; after all, the one gradually evolved from the other in steps that can be reconstructed scientifically. Therefore, a fascinating counterexample to the Social-Darwinist misuse of biology for sociology is the ongoing research into the emergence of cooperation and "altruism" among animals or among self-interested agents in social games. Obviously, individuals by themselves are defined by their biological fitness; on top of that, in their interactions with their kin they start to show signs of altruistic behaviour that by hindsight may be interpreted as "cultural".

In the broadest metaphorical sense, individuals in a population show emergence like atoms in a gas: Each single one behaves according to timeless laws, but collectively they have a history in time. As long as Robinson was alone on his island, day and night, rain and sunshine, the change of tides circled in eternal recurrence. Not until another human being arrived, which he aptly called Friday, did time begin again.

References

Carnap, Rudolf 1999 (org. 128), *Der logische Aufbau der Welt*, Hamburg: Felix Meiner.

Crutchfield, James P. 2012, Between Order and Chaos. In: Nature Physics 8, pp. 17-24.

Mandelbrot, Benoit B. 2000 (Org. 1975), *The Fractal Geometry of Nature*, New York: Henry Holt.

Maynard Smith, John and Szathmáry, Eörs 1995, *The Major Transitions in Evolution*, New York: W. H. Freeman.

Prigogine, Ilya 1980, *From Being to Becoming. Time and Complexity in the Physical Sciences*, New York: W. H. Freeman.

Zeh, H. Dieter 2001, *The Physical Basis of the Direction of Time*, Berlin: Springer.

Lennart Nørreklit

Complexity and practice control
On complexity and construct causality

Introduction

The notion of complexity has been hype in some social contexts recently. In philosophy, the topic of complexity has always been central in one form or another. There are ontological and epistemological perspectives. This paper argues for a practice perspective. The question with which I want to understand this is: What is the function of the concept (in casu complexity) in human construction of reality? What role does this concept play – not only in our understanding, but also in our doing, our living, i.e. in our way of organizing the practice of life? Understanding itself only makes sense in relation to our doing. This question is not to be answered ontologically or epistemologically only, but by a practice-logic that illuminates the role of the notion of complexity in the construction of the practice or life, the role being to manage the intensional relation[1] between acting subject and its surrounding world.

It often appears as if complexity is treated as an almost metaphysical issue neglecting the development of modern philosophy. To avoid this problem the paper first argues that although the world is and has always been very complex, an ontological approach to complexity is not a viable option. In order to study complexity empirically one needs concepts of complexity that presupposed and not constituted by the ontology. The reason why complexity has become an issue is not, that the world has become more complex – although we add to its complexity it has always

---

1 'Intensional' as opposite to 'extensional' - not to be confused with 'intentional'.

been complex – nor that we have discovered its complexity. Therefore neither an epistemological nor the ontological approach will do.

To understand the role of the notions of complexity we have to understand their role in the construction of practice. Thus construction of practice must constitute the framework for understanding the concept. Here we find a dynamic complex of interwoven intensional relationships between epistemological and ontological dimensions of complexity. This enables a distinction between 5 modes of complexity in the analysis of the emergence of a complexity problem.

In order to understand practice one needs to integrate also the dimension of value and of communication in order to provide direction and purpose in the management of the intensional relationships. Through understanding the role of complexity in the construction of practice we may be able to understand why complexity has emerged as a topic. Thus one needs to clarify the type of conditions and functions that are realized by the use of complexity concepts in the construction of practice.

If one misinterprets the role of one's concepts then one entangles oneself in illusions with resulting unpredictable consequences. Thus the article addresses the role of complexity concepts in the endeavors to create control practice. Thus the article integrates complexity concepts in a pragmatic constructivist perspective on construction of reality. In particular the concepts of construct causality and the correlated concept of sufficient reasons are developed and applied in the discussion of complexity. The idea of complexity modes is used to analyze controllability of practice and issues of development and increasing complexity.

Complexity and simplicity – a conceptual complementarity

The concept of complexity is presupposed before we can apply it in say ontology, epistemology or practice. To illuminate the concept we must conceptualize the border between what is and what is not complex. A concept is not understood in itself, but through its relation to other concepts, and a primary relationship may be found through negation. We ask: "what is it that is not complex?" or: "how do we conceptualize that which is not complex?" The term 'complex' seems to contrast concepts such as 'simple', 'single', 'clear'. That something is simple means something like being uncomplicated, easy to manage and find out. Obviously, working with complexity is – logically - working with the relation between the concepts 'complex' and 'simple', and in practice between degrees of complexity: things are always more or less complex or simple. Analysis of complexity without reference to and reflection of simplicity seems logically impossible and thus meaningless. The concepts thus related such as 'complex' and 'simple' are therefore here collectively referred to 'complexity concepts', and the relationship between them is said to form a dimension, the complexity dimension, with the simple in one pole and the complex in the other. It is similar to some degree to the line of natural numbers, starting with 1 in the one end and then having no real finishing largest number in the other direction. One may apply the dimension to different types of phenomena such as, say, things, ideas, problems, etc. i.e. in ontology, epistemology or practice etc.

There seems to exist no absolute standard for something to be simple. It is relative. Although the concept of 'complexity' is understood by the contrast to the 'simple', this contrast is not a sharp either-or – things can be both-and. There are gradual transitions from being (relatively) simple to becoming more and more complex, and eventually be too complex to be clear and simple any longer. There are degrees of complexity and simplicity. The concepts do not form a simple contradictory relationship.

This reference to degrees of complexity, which is obvious in ordinary language, is somehow problematized by an asymmetry between the concepts of simplicity and complexity. On the one hand it is not possible to imagine endless increasing degrees of simplicity – it seems that simplicity has a limit, namely, when we reach something, which is an (absolutely) simple unit, i.e. a unit that cannot be subdivided and analyzed further into parts. This conception of the simple has been the subject of philosophical reflection from Plato's puzzling dialectic of the unity concept in the dialogue *Parmenides*. There is, on the other hand, no logic that indicates that there is a limit to the degree of complexity.

An ontological perspective - realism

Consider first the thesis that complexity is a property of an object or a group of objects or phenomena. Is this thesis meaningful and clear? Is complexity really a possible feature of an object of some sort, a system or structure? Is 'complexity' really a predicate that specifies a sort of property of phenomena or things, such as 'red' or 'heavy'? Or is it a provision belonging to another type of philosophical category, more in the direction of for example 'existence' (as analyzed by say Kant, and Russell), or 'number'? Is it not, to play with the late Wittgenstein, one of the most basic philosophical fallacies of interpreting concepts as a form of *name* so that their meaning is an object they are supposed to refer to?

If we try to interpret complexity ontologically it appears as if we move into an almost pre-Kantian metaphysics somewhat in the direction of rationalist enlightenment. However, it differs from these rationalists in that it emphasizes the complexity pole as primary while the rationalists were concerned with the simplicity pole as primary. Their emphasis on the simplicity pole may be influenced by the scientific ideal coming from the very important emerging natural sciences. In contrast, the actual issue of complexity may consequently be considered a consequence of a crumbling of that ideal of science and modernity influenced of an explosion of an infinite complexity of statistic and other information about society. This development may therefore inspire to look for a perspective beyond enlightenment – i.e. to a Renaissance type of conceptualization. However, the Renaissance responded to the crumbling of the grand Aristotelian synthesis very much with humanistic and constructivist tendencies rather than metaphysics of complexity.

Nevertheless, let us defy the late Wittgenstein and assume that complexity is an object, a phenomenon, with which we are confronted when engaging with the world, i.e. that it is something that is independent of what we do, of our consciousness and independent of whether we want it to be there or not. Thus we presume that the meaning of the concept of complexity is presumed to be some phenomena or objects in the world: the complexes. We apply an ontological realist framework in the interpretation of complexity. Complexity is 'something out there'. It is not something that we form (construct or constitute) through perspectives we apply, but a reality that is forced upon us, because the world is as it is: It *is* complex. 'Complex' denotes a special type of things or phenomena. It is a predicate characterizing certain things and not others. Complexes are certain kinds of things in the world, systems, assemblies, or structures. The whole world may consist of complexes or even the world may be one single large complex. In contrast there are simple units, entities or objects as for example simple substances, sensory data, atoms or quants.

We know, of course, that the world *is* very complex. It has always been that way and human beings have always known this to be true. The complexity of the world cannot, therefore, explain why complexity has become a topic. Something else must explain it. Further, the more we study the world, the more complex it seems to be – we always uncover new complexities. This means that on the one hand there is the complexity, which is known. On the other hand there is the almost infinite complexity, which is not (fully) known, but which exists 'out there' as an incomprehensible complexity of things. This huge complexity is something that we approach with increasing knowledge, but which we never can reach completely. – This we assume although 'complexity' in such absolute meaning is a speculative, metaphysical concept and there is no scientific basis for such type of claim. There is, however, a sound rational *epistemological* interpretation that we might accept instead: One can always *investigate* for deeper complexity. This is a principle to regulate the use of rational reasoning – almost a Kantian regulative principle.

Ontological realism is designed in various ways. Of special interest in relation to complexity is the pluralist-monist dimension. On the one hand, there are pluralistic theories tending towards some form of atomism, according to which *the simple* is the smallest unit that combines to constitute the larger units, the complexes. Politically, this is a basis for an individualistic perspective. Conversely, monism or holistic theories consider that there is a simple holistic unity, which constitutes a complexity of its parts – the parts are not anything in themselves apart from the overarching unity. Politically, it is a basis for a socialist perspective. Pluralism and monism are absolutist perspectives.

Another dimension of interest concerns dualism - the mind-matter relation, or the knowledge-object relation, i.e. an epistemology-ontology relation. Here a very interesting question emerges whether the concepts of complexity behave similarly or differently when applied in ontology or in epistemology.

In contrast to the absolute perspectives there is the relational perspective. Ordinary speaking: "Something is more complicated than something else." Such relational uses of the complexity concepts do not name or characterize a property of an object, they express a comparison. This suggests that complexity is a relativist perspective in which there are neither absolute simple nor absolute complex units, whether monistic or pluralistic, but only units with varying degrees of complexity. - It is obvious that practice applies a relational use of the complexity concepts. A complex is a complex of something that is simpler than the complex it is part of -

without meaning that there must be something that is absolutely simple. Any simple device generally is a complexity of something still simpler. As mentioned, in itself there is no contradiction between being simple and being a complex. Most things are both-and, depending on perspective and context.

A relativistic perspective naturally invites a form of structural approach. This, however, seems to imply possible limits concerning the relativity in the complexity dimension: On the one hand, there are complex units with a given clear structure, which are therefore characterized by an overall simplicity and unity. On the other hand, there are complexities without any clear structure, characterized by dissolution, chaos and lack of transparency – in such cases the perspective of a unity of the complex is lost sight of.

While a relativistic, comparative approach appears unproblematic, absolutistic approaches seem incomprehensible. They treat complexity as a property or phenomenon to be denoted. While a comparison with *respect to various forms of* complexity makes sense, complexity in itself seems unclear: What does complexity look like? We can clearly compare different forms of complexity, for instance complex shape, complex colouring, complex composition etc. – in all cases the complex applies to already given predicates or phenomena, i.e. shape, colour, composition. To call the shape complex does not mean that there is a special form of shape: the complex shape. To call a colouring complex does not mean that there is a special colour called "complex", etc. What we mean by calling something complex appears to be something in this direction: that it cannot be described easily. I.e. it refers to epistemological issues of recognition in relation to the shape or colouring etc. This epistemological interpretation also clarifies the relational usage: that something is more complex than something else - to compare is an act of recognition. For instance that a colouring is more complex than an alternative colouring means that it is more difficult i.e. complex to describe the first than the second colouring. I.e. it has an epistemological connotation.

An epistemological perspective – methodology

The ontological perspective does not illuminate the *function* of the complexity concepts in the construction of the practice of life. Furthermore, it turns out, the apparent ontological references to complex phenomena in reality very much refer to issues of recognition, i.e. they are epistemological references in disguise. Ordinary usage of complexity concepts involves cognitive acts of comparing and no specific aspects of the world in itself.

Methodology

That the world in itself as well as its parts is always complex appears not to be an informative ontological statement but rather a principle of reason to inspire further inquiry. From an epistemological perspective complexity concepts thus seem to be ideals or principles for the use of reason. They embody an idea that leads our search for knowledge – driving an ongoing search for the simple in the complex and the complex in the simple.

This is an analytic principle and a methodological ideal. Descartes developed the ideal in his methodological writings. Here he focused on analyzing the complex down to its logical simple constituent parts in order then to assemble them again in a synthesis. Descartes the rationalist emphasizes *logical* simplicity and thus *logical* complexity, where the logically simple is something that is absolutely clear and distinct and therefore self-evident. Once the logically clear and simple constituents of a complexity are found, one can logically group them again in a synthesis – now the complex is a synthesis and not some fuzzy aggregate. We may add that once that is done the complex synthesis can it seemingly be considered a new type of simple *unit*. The cognitive work of our reason is such a pulsing back and forth between analysis and synthesis to obtain growing insight into increasingly complex relationships.

Descartes was not forced to assume a notion of the existence of complexities that do not constitute a logically ordered synthesis. In a world created by the highest rationality, God, this seemed to be unthinkable.

While the rationalist Descartes considers logically simple and clear ideas as the basis for recognition, the empiricists consider the basis to be simple sensory observations, simple uncompounded sensations or sense data. For a rationalist it is natural to express his ideal in terms of an axiomatic system where axioms express the simple ideas. In contrast empiricism often implies a methodology based on quantitative statistical analysis. Both this form of rationalism and this type of empiricism are kinds of logical atomism.

On the other hand, relativistic, post-enlightenment, and typically system-oriented perspectives interconnect the empirical and the logical as for instance in terms of a gestalt theory, and appear methodologically linked to qualitative depth analysis.

While the enlightenment as well as some of the later absolutistic modern developments took their point of departure in the simple, a complexity inspired approach emphasizes the complex as the point of departure. However, due to the asymmetry described between the concept of the simple and that of the complex this has the consequence that the complex cannot be defined as a system or structure of something simple – because that would be to make the concept of simplicity primary. Thus such perspectives hinge on the problem that complexes would be primary notions without a possible answer to the question: complex of what? The only possible answer would be circular: "complexes of other complexes".

By taking priority in the simple, the epistemological approach of the enlightenment, which outlined modernity, enabled creating modern epistemologies that seemed to imply corresponding rationalist and empiricist ontologies. By rejecting the simple as a possible starting point, the complexity perspective has no access to such approach. Taking complexity as a starting point, without allowing the perspective of deconstructing it into simple constituents, suspends rather than enables rational principles of reflection. Even in a system- and gestalt-perspective the whole has constituents and the relation between whole and constituents is necessary – as in gestalt theory, for instance, a face with no nose, no eyes, no mouth, no forehead, no cheeks, no chin... etc. is no real face.

A central issue relates to the debate on dualism: should a complex be understood as a rational construct of logical relationships or as an empirical construct? Likewise: should a simple unit be understood as locally simple or ontologically simple – or both? Pre-Kantian rationalist enlightenment treats the logical and the empirical as two aspects of the same - as illustrated in Spinoza's double aspect theory. In Kant's epistemology, the two perspectives are not identical as two sides of the same, but they are integrated: Concepts without intuition are empty, they are not about something real; and intuition without concepts is blind, they do not provide understanding.

We reject the idea that the two perspectives on complexity can be two sides of the same. The rationally simple and the empirically simple are not two aspects of the same. Empirically we may not have anything absolutely simple while in logic we operate with simple constituents of a logical system. We are also reluctant that the two sides are always integrated. On the contrary, we believe that we here start to uncover that there is an interplay between the epistemic and the ontological or between the logical and the empirical/factual forms of complexity as a topic of special interest to understanding the *issue* of complexity. Some form of integration between these perspectives is always necessary for the concepts to make sense. In order to observe something, one must necessarily determine that which is observed with *some* concepts. Through this conceptual determination it is automatically linked logically to other concepts. Although we must follow Kant in integrating these perspectives, we shall not merge them in the way he does, only integrate them.

To illustrate my point: *Empirical* simplicity and complexity seems to be something very different from *logical* simplicity and complexity. For example: The rather simple concept 'house' has a certain degree of complexity. However, empirically observed houses appear not only to be very much more complex than the concept of a house, but in addition different houses have very different degrees of complexity – some are small and simple, others are large and very complex. Logical and empirical complexity is not just two sides of the same coin. A double aspect theory does not hold for complexity.

This state of affairs adds extra perspective to the idea that the complexity concepts express a regulative of reason. When applied to *empirical* issues then the complexity concepts function as a kind of eyes or eyeglasses with which we observe and analyze the empirical world. We can always empirically examine something by trying to consider it to be complex in order to find its ingredients and their interrelations. However, when we study the *logical* and *conceptual* complexity we see that the complexity concepts do not function as regulative ideas in the same way. Here we may look for *the simple* as for instance in the form of analytical sentences and self-evident axioms or in simple sense data or simple empirical observations as the mark "x" in a box in a questionnaire.

This asymmetry between the logical and the empirical is a very important fact. It is also a great and fascinating philosophical puzzle that logical constructs such as for instance geometric entities such as geometric points, lines, surfaces and shapes are abstractions that are *not* empirical (you cannot find, measure, see an unextended point, a line with no width or a plane with no thickness), but they are nevertheless used with immense success in empirical practice.

Finally, it must be mentioned that by interpreting the complexity concepts epistemologically as regulative ideas, there emerges the concept of that which we do not know. Thus the *indeterminate* emerges as a new complexity category.

Complexity modes

We shall now describe different modes of interplay between the epistemological (logical/conceptual) and the ontological dimensions of complexity. They may be integrated, or the integration may break down in various ways. This interrelation is significant because it turns out that it creates a dialectic mechanism of development.

We imagine the dimension of complexity ranging from the simple to the complex. At the pole of simplicity is that which is logically simple and clear. At the complexity pole is the extremely complex, which is largely undetermined. It is the world's immense overall complexity. We may conceive this as a logical dimension to structure concepts, or as an empirical dimension to structure things and phenomena that are (amongst other) the objects of our concepts. Ordinarily, however, we do not really distinguish between these – we try to apply clear concepts to the complex world trying to organize things according to their complexity. In this process we actually utilize the asymmetry between these dimensions using relatively simple concepts to grasp and organize complex phenomena. Let us accordingly try to conceptualize the complexity dimension as one operative dimension from a pole of utmost simplicity to a pole of utmost complexity in which the epistemological and the ontological aspects are integrated more or less.

At the simplicity pole, while we rationally may determine simple concepts, it does not appear that such concepts have empirical counterparts. At the other end, the complexity pole, the notion of the extremely or totally complex is itself not a very complex concept although it refers to the greatest complexity, say the total complexity of the world, if not - at least theoretically - even greater complexities.

What is interesting now is to imagine moving along this dimension, from the simple towards the complex. When moving from the logically simple towards the more and more complex we first determine the notion of an organized orderly complex, a *synthesis*. This *is* itself a *simplicity* formed by the *complexity* of underlying units, which in turn may be more or less simple or complex. We are dealing here with a type of clear, well-known and controllable units, which is or enables a functioning system or even practice. We may for instance deal with a living organism. A biological organism is a very complex *synthesis*. The complexity has not dissolved the unity. On the contrary, it forms the functioning unity. Thus, whether a complexity forms a synthesis, a functioning unit, is not a matter of the degree of complexity as such, but a question whether the complexity of the components are sufficiently interrelated to form a clear functionality.

Next comes a kind of complexity that is disorderly although its components are known. They may be tangled together, but they no longer form a synthesis. Such complexity has a convoluted and disjointed structure that it is no longer a functioning unity. We deal with something confusing and uncontrollable. Although one knows all its elements, and although they are interconnected, and the interconnections even are known, there is no functional unity. When for instance society develops and increases the complexity of its legal system this will not in itself prevent the system from making a synthesis. But when the legal system increasingly consists of parts that work in opposite directions, then the system ceases to form a synthesis, a clear functional unit, and it stops working effectively. Although the society of course knows all its laws, i.e. the full complexity of the legal system – if the laws are for instance inconsistent then there is a reduced ability to form a synthesis. The system pulls in opposite directions, no one can predict the overall effect, and the character of the society becomes increasingly fuzzy.

A still further step in the direction of the complexity pole introduces the indeterminate, the unknown complexity. This happens for example when a society or an organization evolves hidden subcultures that cause the emergence of genuine conflicts. Finally at the complexity pole there is the total complex, the world, or an idea of something infinitely complex.

Against this background, we can distinguish between 5 ideal-typical complexity modes (c-modes):

Complexity dimension - 5 ideal-typical C-modes

C1. Logically simple		C2. Complex synthesis		C3. Unstructured complex		C4. Unknown complex		C5. Totality of complex, world
	↔		↔		↔		↔	

C1 is, apparently, only logically and epistemologically interesting. C2, C3 and C4 combine epistemological and ontological complexities. In C2 the simple ideas match the complex reality. In C3 and C4 this is not the case. The relationship between on the one side C2 and on the other C3 and C4 is important in practice, because it is only in C2 practice functions properly, which we shall address in the following but before that we need to address the technical aspects of causality, because that is concerned with the integration of the epistemic and the ontological aspects.

Technology and construct causality

Practice is about to get things to work. That requires controlling the effect of processes, i.e. control of causal relations. For this purpose practices use technology. Modern technology is largely formed in accordance with the Cartesian concept for analysis and synthesis. Analytical conceptual models outlining technical system are implemented in physical science-based technologies – i.e. a piece of working technology exemplifies complexity mode C2.

Now, technological systems are complex constructions of interrelated causal relations. Such causal relations are technical constructs that form a mechanism of the type: *If* A is done, *then* B happens. Such a technological causal sequence is created. It is constructed: *construct causality*. It is *not* a law of nature described in a textbook in physics. And yet it is based on an application of recognized physical laws. An example: 'If I press the letter 'k' on my keyboard, then 'k' appears on my monitor'. This expresses a causal relationship. Good things about it are that it is reliable, and that I control the cause – thus I am in control of the effect. Modern life rests throughout on constructed causality. Construct causalities serve the construction of new possibilities. The actor can choose whether to enact the initial triggering cause or not. Therefore the technical systems of construct causalities provide the actors with possibilities that could not be achieved without them. This construction of possibilities is the purpose of technology.

When the pressure on the key can cause the occurrence of a character on the monitor, it is because a number of intermediate causal links have been constructed. There is a long transitive chain of causal relations, which connect the pressure on the k-key with the letter occurring on the monitor. The *simple* constructed causal relationship that a press on the k-key implies the letter 'k' to be written on the screen is a summary of a very *complex* set of constructed causal relations connecting the two events. The simple causal relation is a synthesis of a complex string of intermediate constructed causal steps – it embodies mode C2. There can of course be all sorts of problems in this construction that will cause the causal relation to collapse: the electricity can e.g. be switched off, there may have come juice in the keyboard, the connection with the display may have been turned off, etc. The construction must be in order. But if it is okay then there is a working causal relationship: Pressing the key implies - in the sense of 'causes' - the corresponding letter to appear on the monitor. The implication is not that of a logical consequence but a constructed empirical causal relation.

There is no law of nature in textbooks on physics saying: 'A press on the k-button causes the letter 'k' to appear on the monitor'. Thus the causality here is not of the same type as described in the covering law model, which requires that a law of nature and not a human construct determines the connection between cause and effect. Yet, at the basis of our immensely complex technology, there are relatively few and simple natural laws based on a small number of fundamental forces of nature. While there are countless technological constructed causal relations in use in daily practice, there are only few fundamental natural forces.

For example, consider a mechanical watch, which one can analyze and come apart into a number of components. The clock is a complexity. There are gears, screws, springs, etc. These are its simple physical components as seen with a watchmaker's eyes. He does for instance not perceive such watch as composed of atoms. He has conceptualized these physical components in a unified model of a logical-empirical synthesis: a model of the functioning clock. When the parts are assembled accordingly, it is a synthesis of a complex, embodying mode C2. The different component parts are characterized, however, still further, the spring has certain strength, the gears have a certain diameter and a plurality of thank etc. etc. They are therefore also complex syntheses. The watchmaker even uses a certain level of elementary geometry and physics - here is an element of applied science.

The watchmaker thus uses the distinction simple-complex on a practical physical level. However, it is unlikely that he uses the same level of simplicity, as Descartes considered basic, i.e. C1. The level of analysis used by the watchmaker is C2 as determined by the requirements in practice. Descartes' level is determined by the quest for logically clear conceptual insight. To achieve logically clear and simple understanding, Descartes would for example demand simple geometric formulae to analyze the wheels and other components completely. First then the analysis reaches the level of clear self-evident concepts. Here the distinction simple-complex is anchored in absolute simplicity, so to speak. All that is not necessary for the watchmaker. He may not understand the circle logically. Nevertheless, understanding the underlying geometry crucial for technological development; and the separation between applied science and basic science is not as clear today as in the above context of the mechanism clock.

This underscores the interesting condition that the asymmetry in the dimension of complexity holds true only for epistemological purposes, logic, concept formation and methodology, but *not* in a context of ontology or practice. Ontologically speaking, it is conceivable and in practice it seems to be a fact that there is no absolute limit for simplicity, as there seems to be none for complexity. In practice, simplicity is always a synthesis of a complex, that is, a state of type C2 (not of C3 or C4, because they lack the synthesis necessary to be a simplicity).

Why this is so? The answer is, I think, that concepts are something we construct. This construction can be guided by ideals of reason. It is natural that for instance clarity and reliability function as such ideals - whether we address issues of recognition and knowledge, or whether we are concerned with applying knowledge in practice. In order to obtain knowledge that is clear and certain, clear concepts are needed. This leads to the ideal of logical clarity and simplicity pertaining to our concepts. Without clear and simple concepts clear conceptual thinking is not possible. Clear concepts are not obtained automatically through linguistic tradition. On the contrary. Otherwise there would have been no need for philosophy and science. Clear concepts are created through a reflexive processing of the vague and ambiguous concepts of tradition. This processing leads to sharpened concepts, development of new concepts, and corresponding refinements of language. Sciences develop their own conceptual systems and corresponding languages. These languages and conceptual systems are usually characterized by the asymmetric ideal in that there are a number of basic concepts that complex structures are determined from.

It is obvious that construct causality presupposes that the technical complex embodies a clear conceptualized synthesis. There is a clear logical as well as empirical connection from a press on the button to the letter on the monitor. It is embedded logically in the design of the computer systems and it is empirically realized in a constructed transitive string of causal relations. Complex technology consists in the design of complex syntheses of causative constructions. It realizes complexities in C2 mode. In C2 the cognitive, conceptual synthesis fits the factual synthesis of the empirical manifold.

Practice perspective

Concepts must be defined in relation to their role in practice - otherwise they create dreams and illusions rather than reality. The idea of a purely theoretical, non-practice related knowledge seems speculative. Language and concepts can only be understood in relation to their use – and their use is their role in the construction of the reality by the language using actors. Language does of course not work alone – reality, the world is not just language. Practice is not just talk. For instance, people have needs – however, they cannot eat language.

Thus complexity is defined in an epistemological or ontological perspective, but in its role in shaping and maintaining *practice*. This comprises but cannot be reduced to epistemological or ontological issues. The issue of complexity in practice addresses technological action as well as functioning in organized interaction. Whether something is complex or simple is primarily a question whether it is a simple or complex matter for the actor to find out and to handle.

In order to establish and drive a viable functioning practice the use of language must integrate rational recognition with empirical reality, i.e. epistemology and ontology must be integrated. The use of the complexity perspective in the formation of concepts and models (syntheses) must be related to its use in analyzing the practical objects – as outlined in the model of complexity modes. By integrating the empirical facts with concepts and logic, a world of alethic modalities, i.e. of necessities / impossibilities and especially possibilities is created. If the logical structures are not integrated in the factual, then neither factual possibilities nor impossibilities can be recognized. Thus no practice can be conceived let alone be created. By setting up technical systems of construct causalities, the integration of facts and logic produces advanced new possibilities.

It is not only the empirical/factual aspects that must be integrated in order for practice to function. They must be integrated in a common language that connects people and enables them to control practice. Further it is necessary also to integrate values so that the potential values of the actors lie within the factual possibilities. Otherwise people do not have sufficient reasons to act, and the necessary motive and force will be weak.

Intensional links – theory and practice

In order to analyze complexity in relation to practice one has to introduce the acting person, the actor. In so far as he/she is designing and constructing the system of practice or the string of causalities used, we refer to the constructor. Actor and constructor are not sharply separated, thus there is an overlap in our usage. I shall sometimes use 'actor' as also comprising constructors. Actors relate to a topic they address as in expressions such as 'A does B', 'A sees B', etc. Let us call such relations between a person and a topic for *intensional,* an *intensional link.* The terms 'actor' and 'constructor' emphasizes the presence of an active element in the intensional relations in that the person influences the topic, in distinction to terms such as 'human being', 'person' or especially 'subject' that are neutral or even point out a passive element in the intensional relation. I consider the lack of an active element in a person's life as inadequate to human nature and therefore a form of suffering. However, periods of activity must be combined with periods of impression, experience and reflection – i.e. a cycle of withdrawal and return (cf. John MacMurray[2]).

The actor has already implicitly been introduced as subject through the epistemic perspective. Let this therefore be the starting point. Consider the dialogue fragment, a slice of a possible epistemic language game:

A: What is the answer to the question X?
B: It's too complicated, I cannot figure it out.
A: No, it's really *simple* - the solution is Y.
B: Do you *know* if it is the true answer?
A: Yes, of course. It is *obvious* / self-evident.

---

2   John MacMurray 1957, *The self as agent*, London: Faber & Faber. However, I use the terms 'actor' and 'constructor' instead of 'agent'. Agents are people acting on behalf of others.

The fragment expresses a string of intensional relations. It is clear that the terminology concerning complexity concepts is related to recognition. This may not be explicit, but it is true implicitly, as illustrated in the fragment. 'Complex' means that the recognition is difficult to the person, 'simple' that it is not or should not be difficult to the person. Epistemic concepts such as belief and knowledge etc. are not extensional but intensional: They are not only concerned with the subject matter, they do also – explicitly or implicitly - refer to the people that are assumed to believe or know. Here the basic concern is the link between the epistemic subject and the subject matter as expressed in the formula 'A knows/believes that B'. In so far as this intensional link is concerned with epistemic issues, we may call it a *cognitive link*.

The fragment above illustrates that complexity concepts also are concerned with the links between person and subject matter. They are intensional concepts. Further, they are obviously part of the cognitive links between person and subject matter. Thus, whether something is complex is relative not only in the sense that a phenomenon or state is more or less complex than another state, but also in the sense that complexity concerns the *cognitive links* between a perceptive being and some state of affairs. Complexity is not just an attribute of the object, nor a relation between objects; it is an intensional determination of the links between a subject and its object (for instance an organization or society). Thus it is misleading to consider complexity concepts as expressions of special objects, neither properties nor external relations only.

Considering complexity concepts as cognitive intensionality links raises the question, how the complex system of cognition of the subject relates to the complexities of the subject matter, the topic or object? It is as if the link projects a complexity in both directions, the subject as well as the subject matter. The result is expressed in an intensional statement such as 'This is simple' or 'This is complex'. Suppose for instance A says: 'B is simple'. Here the word 'simple' tells that the topic B is somehow easy *to A* – without specifying whether B is in itself simple or complex. But, comparatively, if A says, 'C is complex', meaning, that C is complex from A's perspective, not in itself. Nevertheless, if B and C are comparable, then this would lead us to expect that C *in itself* in some respect is more complex than B. But, whether B and C are considered as simple or complex depends not only on their complexities but also on the level of knowledge of the subject. Thus there is no reason to believe that complexity provisions allow a direct mapping of the object without any understanding of the level of knowledge presupposed. Complexity means complex for someone or something - a person, an organization, or a society.

There is an important difference between cognitive links such as 'A believes that B' and 'A knows that B'. 'A believes that B' tells nothing about B in itself. It only characterizes A. However, 'A knows that B' not only gives us information about A it also provides information about the world, namely, that B is the case. Let us express this by saying that belief statements have no extensional consequence, knowledge statements do have extensional consequence. I.e.: The intensional knowledge statement "A knows that P" does not only express information about A, it also has the consequence, that the extensional (non-intensional) statement P is true. On the other hand, the intensional belief statement "A believes that P" has no consequence regarding the truth of P, it only states something about A. The question is then: do complexity statements have extensional impact? When C is more complex than B to A, this might lead us to expect a higher degree of complexity in C than in B and thus conclude that complexity has an ontological meaning. Still, we are confronted with a puzzling issue. Remembering the argument, that for instance complex colour is not a new colour, the colour complexity, etc. creates a discomfort about the realist interpretation and makes it seem more reasonable to claim that complexity concepts do not directly have extensional impact. On the other hand there is nevertheless an extensional element, systems are more or less complex, and this complexity may be understood or not understood by the actor. Still to call the system complex appears to be informative in relation to the conceptualization of the system only. In itself, everything is just simply complex.

The complexity modes seem directly to be expressions of the character of the intensional complexity links. In C2 the subject can grasp and control the complexity. The subject can have relatively simple concepts to control the complex practice. In C3 this is not possible. Although the subject should know all the details about the complex units, they cannot be synthesized – there is not cognitive deficit but an inadequate system. It is like all the parts of a watch not being assembled. In C4 the subject is ignorant about important issues of the complexity concerned, there is a cognitive deficit. The subject knows there is something, but has no concept to interpret it.

The cognitive issues have a purpose, i.e. to enable and control practice, i.e. designing and controlling complex strings of construct causalities. In mode C2, the actor is in control. The complex system functions because the causal strings are set up properly, and the concepts and models of the actors understand this function sufficiently to enable control by enacting the causal strings. C3 and C4 on the other hand involve loss of control. The conceptualization of the complexity and the complexity of the system must match in order to enable control. Control involves two things: ability purposely to enact the initial causes in the strings of construct causalities and the functioning of these strings.

Problems relating often labeled as problems of theory and practice address the problem of establishing a proper intensional linking in establishing and maintaining the C2 mode, i.e. a proper interaction between the cognition and the causal system necessary. Inadequacies of the intensionale complexity-link trigger a variety of so-called theory-practice problems. When the mode of the complex changes from C2 to C3 or C4 then the actor is faced with complexes, which do not form a structured whole, which he/she can control. Technology stops working effectively. Practice slows down or may not work at all.

Crucial to practice is not the question whether complex or not so complex - complexity is always involved. Decisive to practice is whether the complex forms a synthesis – i.e. whether it is a C2 unit or not. Crucial is the type of mode of the complex. Through the development of high complexity practice therefore is threatened by two problems: the problem that the complex does not form a whole synthesis, i.e. the various sub-complexes act in different directions, resulting in unpredictable consequences (cf. C3); and the problem that the complex is influenced by unknown relationships with unknown effects, which can therefore not be taken into account (cf. C4). The last is characteristic, as one moves over into a new area.

There are other problems associated with the intensional structure of complexity in practical systems. The transition from concept to observable practice involves loss of precision. There are always degrees of uncertainty in observation and measurement. This leads to uncertainty regarding the effects of the endeavors to control. Thus a high degree of complexity poses a risk that completely unexpected effects emerge (cf. chaos theory). In such situations the actor has *theoretically* a complexity in a C2 mode, but in real *practice* it is in a C4 mode, and control becomes uncertain.

Furthermore, the act of recognition itself is a form of practice. As such, it affects the more encompassing practice, of which it is a sub-practice, but which it is used to control. But it influences the encompassing practice in ways it cannot fully predict. Thus the very endeavor to create control through knowledge creates in itself unpredictable consequences. This is an issue in philosophy as well as a general issue in most methodology, but often not recognized in practice. The more elaborate and complex the system of recognition is that is used to control the practice, the more unpredictable its effects may be.

Hype- and hyper-complexity

The term hyper-complexity can be interpreted in various ways. On the one hand, it can point in the direction of *hyper-reality*, i.e. in the direction of reality constructions that present also fictions even illusions as reality[3]. Thus hyper-complexity resembles the idea of reality as a simulacrum. It involves illusions. Hyper-complexity is a state of types C3 and C4, basically possibly mistaking it for a normal state, because one assumes that complexity is purely ontological and not intensional.

On the other hand, the prefix '*hype*' points in the direction of enthusiasm, high energy, something that is 'in' or 'hot'. These two interpretations are to some extent related – they can support and counteract each other. That something is hype is associated with ideas of something being new, a new synthesis or identity, from which a lot is to be expected. Often these enthusiastic and aroused expectations are not based on special insight that supports these expectations; rather it comes from an energy created through belonging to a special and easily identifiable community. Hyper-complexity in practice involves pseudo-causal relationships, causal relations that are not realistic, because they are not shorthand of any viable transitive chain of causal relations.

Management of a practice may be tempted to try to create extra energy behind an initiative by seeking to make it hype for employees. Such hype may simply be an illusion of performing something great or special. The motivating pep talks may just be simulacra, i.e. a hyper-reality. Usages of

---

3   Hyper reality are reality constructs where people resort to social constructs of language neglecting credible observations - cf. from Plato (The Sophist) over Nietzsche (*The Twilight of the Idols*) to Baudrillard and Deleuze & Guattaris' notions of simulacrum.

the term 'hyper-complexity' may itself carry such illusion. The reason why managers and leaders instigate such hype is that by making a project hype, they can create so much energy behind the project that it may *become* realistic by overcoming its initial character of hyper-reality. This may however easily appear to be an abuse of employees - the company does not live by the work but the enthusiasm of the workers. It should be the other way round: enthusiasm is due to a good project; not: the poor project is 'made good' because of the enthusiasm. One might even generally consider whether stress is an expression of the facts that what is presented to employees as a hype complex, in reality is a hyper-complex i.e. something that does not have credibility – thus people try to work very hard to reach an impossible goal. People are made to run to the pseudo targets by creating such enthusiasms – these goals are both hype and hyper.

The use of creating hype reveals that enthusiasm plays a role in the causal relations. This finally leads us to the issue of supplementing the intensional integration of factual complexity with cognition with integrating *values*.

Actors and sufficient reasons

Mostly control problems are, however, avoided because the organization consists of actors that automatically observe deviations and emerging problems and automatically take counter measures. It is flexibility in the control of practice that enables competent actors to compensate deviances in the strings of construct causalities. The reason behind this approach is that the constructors *are* motivated by sufficient reasons to do so and that they have the necessary skills to act relatively independent.

So far we have, however, been concerned with integrating the cognitive and the factual in constructing the intensional complexity mode. We need to blend in values and communication in this integration. The problems discussed so far are related to this restriction. We could consider it the restriction where the perspective is that of technology, of applied classic natural science, a combination of theory and facts, of the rational and the empirical. But this perspective does not only result in the problems mentioned, it also mistreats people as passive or reactive, as if they themselves were technological units, machines.

Furthermore, it is necessary to integrate values in the integrated construct of facts and logic. For practice to function, the actors must be motivated which presupposes that their values are within the range of factual possibilities. Otherwise, actors cannot find sufficient reason to act according to the conditions of the practice constructed. Consequently they will not experience the necessary motive and drive.

A person participating in practice is an actor. The actors that set up practice and create the strings of construct causalities are the constructors. Life world is not proceeding as it does by itself, because the causality, which shapes the world, is not only given by nature – it is constructed based on the given and natural conditions. To control practice it is therefore essential to understand people as constructors *and* actors, including understanding the role, which concepts, including the complexity concepts, play in the process. If one analytically tries to reduce the model for control to a purely technological model, as we implicitly have done so far then one also eliminates the role of human constructors and actors that produce and use the technology, and reduce them to being themselves technological instruments, robots.

In order to be able to act, people need a *factual* basis, which integrates *possibilities* for action – i.e. action presupposes *factual possibilities*. Otherwise, endeavours to act fail. Furthermore, people must have values to motivate and drive it, which lies within the range of the factual possibilities. Values outside the range of factual possibilities do not motivate the actions in question. However, if the values are within the scope of factual possibilities then man has a *sufficient reason* to act and he/she will realize the goal because it is within the range of the actor's possibilities. Thus this is the recipe for success.

People attempt to construct concepts that enable them to act successfully and achieve their goals. I.e. their basic concepts must integrate their facts, possibilities and values in order to enable them to make up a sufficient reason, so that they can determine and decide their actions.

To establish a social practice, it is necessary that there is a common language in which the reasons of all the participants can be reflected and sufficient reasons made up for each. The reflection aims at formulating a synthesis that is supported by a conceptual control topos, which enables the people involved to find sufficient reason for their participation.

Practice needs more than technical constructed causalities. For instance the technical causalities need to be constructed and used. This means that the activity of one person brings another person to act. Technological construct causality is supplemented with a social form of causality. Practice contains endless strings of social causalities. This type of causal relationship is not causal in the technical or physical sense. It depends not only on the skills and competences of the individuals, but also on their willingness and attitude, which is based on their personal values. These social causations are the realization of sufficient reasons of the actors. The fact that one person acts becomes and is meant to become a sufficient reason for another person to act. If people do not find that there is a sufficient reason then one cannot expect them to act accordingly. It does not suffice that some person, for example the boss, believes that there is sufficient reason for the employee to act. It is necessary that they who are supposed to act perceive that they have sufficient reason to do so. It must be *their* reasons. Thus, an organization must be driven by continuous convincing communication that establishes sufficient reasons for action from all the participants. Control of practice is therefore necessarily a common concern involving all participants.

It is the inclusion of values and the ability to create sufficient reasons that changes the intensional link between the person and his/her world from being a purely epistemic relation to become a practice relation in which the person becomes an actor. The system of reasons that organizes practice is also a construct. All parties involved participate in this construction through which the participants either obtain or do not obtain sufficient reasons to participate and cooperate.

Thus we need to interpret construct causality in a wider sense. On the one hand, technical construct causality is concerned with construction of strings of physical causal relations. On the other hand social or organizational construct causality is about setting up a system of sufficient reasons that make the participants cooperate to realize the purpose of the practice concerned. [4]

In a complex organization the knowledge of the many constructed causal relations is distributed amongst the participants. An organization therefore finds itself in a complexity mode that in a sense is an intermediate between C2 and respectively C3. On the one hand, all the operating causal relations are known and coordinated from the given identity – they constitute a synthesis, i.e. mode C2. On the other hand, this

---

4   It is important to distinguish between reasons and physical causes. – Yet there is a need for a common denominator. One cannot evade mutual and managerial responsibilities for creating sufficient reasons for participants under the heading that causal relations are mechanical or deterministic.

knowledge is not in one place, but distributed in the organization. Thus different parties may pull in opposite directions, if they are led by incompatible motives. Such things can be caused by many different factors, such as the meeting of different cultures, that the communication does not work, that there are hidden contractual obligations or objectives, etc. - i.e. the organization enters mode C4. It is imperative that the management organizes a topos that provides guidelines for the construction of a system of sufficient reasons so that operations can be efficient and conflicts avoided.

Development and change

Complexity is necessary to create possibilities for practice and complexity can destroy possibilities and create impossibilities in practice. To possess possibilities the complexities of practice must embody mode C2. It must be a synthesis including a conceptual topos to control the many causal and motivational relationships.

It is normal that a society or an organization becomes more and more complex as time passes. The guiding imagination may be that possibilities improve with increased complexity. But: increased complexity can have the opposite effect. Increasing complexity is a problem if it undermines the synthesis, so it no longer can function according to its purpose. It is not the complexity but the changes in the relation between synthesis and complexity that causes problems.

In a dialectic perspective development is typically characterized as a quantitative change, which causes a thesis to turn into its opposite, an anti-thesis, which then is followed by a qualitatively new synthesis. The present complexity perspective forms a slightly different description of development: Development is a process driven by the fact that governance of companies and communities normally solve problems by increasing complexity in practice. When problems are observed new laws and regulations are introduced. Thus the practice becomes more and more complex until finally it is hyper-complex. The complexity mode is no longer C2 but C3 or C4. It gradually gets less and less clear whether practice still realizes the basic synthesis or not. Development is increasingly characterized by unforeseen side effects; rules counteract each other and include exceptions that make them opaque, etc. The control tools lose effect.

In the attempts to regain command and control modern management increasingly applies behavioral procedures and controls that precisely in all detail prescribe what employees should do in every situation. Through this development the use of sufficient reason, which are based on respect and regard for the actor's skills and values, motivation and competence, is replaced by *dictates* that regulate behavior, disregards the actor's independence, and discharges his need for sufficient reasons as irrelevant. In this way leadership overrules actors as people. Unethically, management of people is handled as if it was commanding robots. The idea behind it is apparently that problems arise because the players do not do what they are supposed to do - and not because the management is inadequate. The effect of this is of course low management effectiveness, which leads to a constant need to develop new rules and regulations that increase complexity. It dismantles the actor's intensional link, and social pathological problems increase.

As an example, consider the effect of the communist plan-economic governance. In itself plan-economy was a rational concept. But the system created a rule complexity, which eventually strangled the system, replaced it with an underground economy that finally abolished the system. Another example is the ever-growing volume of legislation in developed capitalist democracies, in which all the laws are constantly reformed all the time - apparently because none of them are able to resolve the problems they address satisfactorily. [5] Ideally, these economies aim at solving such problems by letting the markets eliminate units that are no longer competitive. This resolution mechanism is, however, also countered by the development of social complexity, which increasingly controls the market. It may be this problem of hyper-complexity that produces the present interest in complexity.

Thus new management initiatives lose ability to achieve intended effect the more the practice system moves away from a C2 mode. The legal framework gets difficult to manage even using large amounts of legal and financial administrative skills available everywhere the rules apply. The introduction of new rules progressively loses its ameliorative effect. And since new measures do not immediately function as intended, one

---

5   A case: In 2010, the Danish trade union *Min A-Kasse* illuminated the complexity problem by creating the world's biggest book, 23,675 pages, consisting solely of rules concerning the governance of unemployment support. – The amount of regulation is growing so fast that people cannot keep up with it.

constantly re-improves them. The development seemingly implies ongoing reduction of the time horizon of the effects of new management actions - a process whose end is not in sight.

The problem of hyper-complexity cannot be solved in a defined unit only – in one country, one institution or company. The system is global and development cannot be made to go backwards. What can be done in situations of complexity is, *in principle*, to develop a new kind of synthesis in relation to which there can be established a new integrated, and thus effective control topoi can be established, which can organize a system of sufficient reasons based on a new understanding of the organization. That requires very new penetrative thinking. However, the resources for generating such new perspectives, i.e. science and philosophy, are themselves in the service of the system and subject to its control. And it detests real change. Therefore, it is unlikely that a new viable synthesis, which is capable to overcome the existing system, will emerge in the near future.

There is always some flashing of new ideas to reassurance of critics. But it is difficult to spot the necessary power behind emerging new ideas. [6] It is therefore to be expected that the trend to increase hyper-complexity continues, until the development blocks itself or is hit by one of the global problems at the horizon.

---

6   We recall Obama's agenda in the election campaign: 'change' and 'yes we can'. It is difficult to imagine how to organize a greater force of change. And what happened?

References

Baudrillard, Jean, 1994, *Simulacra and Simulation*, Ann Arbor: University of Michigan Press.

Deleuze, Gilles & Guattari, Félix, 1968, *Difference and Repetition*, New York: Columbia University Press.

Descartes, René, 1966, *Regulae ad Directionem Ingenii* 1626-28, The Hague: Martinus Nijhoff.

Kant, Immanuel, 1787, *Kritik der reinen Vernunft*, Riga: Johann Friedrich Hartknoch.

Macmurray, John, 1957, *The self as Agent*, London: Faber&Faber.

Nietzsche, Friedrich, 1984, *Götzendämmerung*, Frankfurt a. M.: Suhrkamp.

Plato 2008, *Parmenides*, Rockville: Arc Manor.

Plato 1996, *Plato's Sophist. The Professor of Wisdom,* Translation and introduction by Eva Brann, Peter Kalkavage, Eric Salem, Newburyport: Focus Publishing.

Russell, Bertrand, 1905, "On Denoting", 1905. In R. Marsh, 1956, *Logic and Knowledge: Essays 1901–1950*, London: George Allen and Unwin, pp. 39–56.

Wittgenstein, Ludwig, 1953, *Philosophical Investigations,* Oxford: Basil Blackwell.

Søren Willert

The Natural History of Memory
An essay in complexity theory

Introduction (1): Background

My process of getting acquainted with the complexity viewpoint started only a few years ago – but late in my professional life as a university-based psychologist-practitioner. In a practical vein, the complexity viewpoint added new perspectives to my understanding of organizational life and the consultant's potential role as helper (chapters 3-4 in Søholm & Willert 2010). In an intellectual vein, it helped me build bridges between theoretical positions/traditions that had hitherto seemed to me mutually antagonistic.

Part of this bridge building concerned a heightened sense of natural historical continuity between the three ontological realms of (1) non-living (prebiotic) matter, (2) biosphere and (3) human life worlds respectively. This sense of continuity contrasted sharply with a physicalist world view. Physicalism poses an absolute discontinuity between pre-biotic matter and biosphere, thereby making the transition from non-living matter to biosphere an enigma – unless you opt for some sort of vitalism or choose to call in an intelligent designer.[1]

Opposition to physicalism most often derives from intellectual or professional cultures with no active commitment to natural scientific research in the classical sense. The complexity theory version presented in this article developed as part of physical science – but subjects data from this research tradition to partial reinterpretation. This reinter-

---

1 These issues are discussed in Gregersen 2003.

pretation implies a softening of the strict discontinuity between pre-biotic matter and biosphere. According to complexity theory certain operative principles, which, normally, we regard as quintessentially biological, i.e. life- or bio-sphere-sustaining, did not have to be invented all anew when nature was ready to start constructing the biosphere. Examples:

- The complexity state known as 'the edge of chaos' produces so-called strange attractors, i.e. movement trajectories that defy predictability by developing constantly new (non-recurring) patterns no matter how long the observation period is extended. Such strange attractors are pre-biotic analogues to the principle of historicity governing social development (Marion 1999).
- Pre-biotic matter in states far from dynamic equilibrium is known to develop short-lived structural patterns, so-called dissipative structures that defy the second law of thermodynamics and cannot be explained with reference to linear causality (Prigogine 1997).
- Memory is a third conceptual candidate for bridge building between pre-biotic matter and bio-sphere. Memory-like phenomena, or generalized: time-binding,[2] not only exists in lifeless matter, its existence is known to have important practical consequences for the way reality works.

This, then, is the reason why, early during my complexity studies, "A Natural History of Memory" emanated as an appealing title for an essay. Natural history of memory is my account of memory's transition from relatively simple ('un-intelligent') pre-biotic forms to much more elaborate, life-sustaining forms found at the two 'higher' ontological levels mentioned. Most attention will be given to the pre-biotic realm, because this is the part of the story least known.

Introduction (2): Structure of paper

My aim in what follows is not just to present the natural history of memory as a scientific knowledge field. I also trace the historical devel-

---

2   From now on I shall use 'time-binding' as a generalized designation of the operative principle behind memory manifestations.

opment of this field. The development process was a long one. As is the case for many knowledge fields, its origins are found in Ancient Greece. The tension between viewing the world as essentially stable (Parmenides ca. 525-450 BC) or rather viewing it as essentially in flux (Heraclitus, ca. 535-475 BC) is part of our culture's Pre-Socratic heritage and this tension has been endemic to Western history of ideas ever since. Thus, the first instalment in my presentation of the natural history of memory deals with Epicurus' (341-270 BC) decision to add a Heraclitic twist (random fluctuation) to the essentially Parmenidean cosmology developed by Democritus (ca. 460-370 BC). Epicurus' intervention was philosophically motivated, as a means toward bridge-building between necessity and freedom and introduced complexity as a legitimate aspect of the world. Nothing in his intervention pointed at complexity as being based on processes of a memory-like nature. More than two thousand years should pass before that notion surfaced.

The second instalment in my story line has the French mathematician Jules Henri Poincaré (1854-1912) as its hero. Late in the 19th century Poincaré had been busy trying to solve a burdensome problem in celestial mechanics (movements of the heavenly bodies). The world-as-observed seemed to possess degrees of freedom that were not 'allowed' by Newtonian mechanics, i.e. by the Parmenidean hard-liner theory of his day. As will appear, Poincaré's modifications of Newtonian mechanics show some striking formal similarities to Epicurus' above-mentioned Heraclitic additions to Democritus' atomic conception of Cosmos. Differences are also to be noticed, however – and these differences are exactly what allows us to understand the dynamics of complexity as partly being brought about by memory-like processes.

Poincaré's contributions were of a theoretical nature based on mathematical reasoning. The next breakthrough in my 'Natural History'-narrative comes when digital computers had made it possible (during the 1960s and onward) to do actual observations of (simulated copies of) real-life scenarios equivalent to those referred to in Poincaré's differential equations. The advent of computers formed the technological background for empirical investigations of chaos and complexity phenomena, with Ilya Prigogine (1917-2003) as one important contributor. The third installment of my narrative presents a simple version of the real-world effects following from the universal presence of time-binding (memory) at all reality levels.

In the fourth installment of my narrative I make a summary of the role played by memory and other complexity-based real-world aspects in adaptive, evolutionary processes of the animal kingdom. This installment revolves around well-known biological functions. They are presented so as to draw the reader's attention to functional continuities all the way from pre-biotic reality to bio-sphere and onward to the realm of human life-worlds.

Fifth installment deals with the human realm and with the peculiar consequences following from human beings' unique capacity for objectifying (or 'environmentalizing') their own life-sustaining interactivity with their natural environments.

Finally, given that reflections on determinism versus the power of human volition played an important role as meta-scientific motivation for complexity researchers, these issues will be touched upon in the article's sixth and concluding installment.[3]

Epicurus' Heraclitic Modification of Democritus' Atomism

The first chapter in Prigogine's *The End of Certainty* (1997) is called *Epicure's dilemma*. Here Prigogine tells the story of Epicurus who, as an intellectual reformer, was drawn towards the 'modern' cosmological ideas of Democritus. These ideas were launched as a replacement for the 'old-fashioned' belief in personified gods as benevolent caretakers of individuals and communities. At the same time Epicurus felt discomfort when confronted with the merciless determinism of Democritus' cosmological model. According to this model the elementary building blocks of matter, named atoms (literally: indivisibles), moved along their predetermined courses leaving no room for the emergence of situation-based novelty, let alone influences from human, change-oriented actions. In a letter to a friend, Epicurus ironically commented that the prospect of merciless determinism seemed to him so distasteful, that it might even make him revert to that religious frame of mind he wished to leave behind: "Our will is autonomous and independent and to it we can attribute praise or disapproval. Thus, in order to keep our freedom, it

---

3 After having finished the writing process I came across Deacon, 2012, which deals, in a most inspiring way, with transitions between the same three ontological realms as form the basic structure of this essay.

would have been better to remain attached to the belief in gods rather than being slaves to the fate of the physicists: The former gives us the hope of winning the benevolence of deities through promise and sacrifice; the latter, on the contrary, brings with it an inviolable necessity." (from Prigogine 1997: 10)

Not only did Democritus' model seem unsavory to Epicurus. It also appeared counter-intuitive. On the one hand many events rolled along with what seemed like necessity. On the other hand, unpredictable novelty also occurred in the world as we know it. And most importantly: Individual human beings did have the capacity to intervene, at times successfully, with a view to restructure event sequences that went against their desire as known to them.

Based on considerations such as these Epicurus saw fit to add unpredictable chance elements to the courses followed by atoms. In that way he tried to bridge the gap between Parmenidean (world as essentially stable) and Heraclitic (world as essentially in flux) world views. O'Keefe (2005: 1) has this summary:

> " ... if all atomic motions were the deterministic result of past motions and weight, we would not have the 'free volition' (libera voluntas) which allows each of us to move ourselves as we wish. Since we evidently do have the power to move ourselves as we wish there must be a third, indeterministic cause of atomic motion, in addition to weight and motions – a swerving of the atoms to the side at uncertain times and places, which save us from fate."

Roughly 2.000 years later Epicure's dilemma was re-enacted by Prigogine. In *The End of Certainty* (1997) he describes how, in his formative years, he had felt stifled from having to live in a world supposedly functioning according to strict (merciless) determinism. Determinism repudiated the potency of human action and seemed counter-intuitive. He decided to become a student of natural science hoping to discover ways of reshaping its foundational structure so that it made room for historicity, i.e. emergence of novelty as a function of time.[4]

---

4   The post-humously published *Is Future Given?* (Prigogine 2003) contains relatively non-technical discussions on complexity phenomena and their possible implications for human self-understanding.

Epicurus had nothing but himself and his intuition to guide him when he decided to add unpredictable swerving to the courses followed by atoms. Prigogine and the research community dealing with chaos and complexity found an equivalent to Epicurean swerving in physico-mathematical analyses done by Poincaré prior to 1900 as part of his efforts to solve the so-called three-body problem.

Poincaré and the Three-body Problem

The three-body problem had been registered by Newton in his *Principia*. Since then, it had been considered a threat to Newtonian mechanics, theoretically as well as practically, in that it violated the *principle of linearity* stating that 'the whole equals the sum of its parts'. The *theoretical* problem consisted in the lack of adequate mathematical tools to predict the movement of an aggregate with more than two components based on movement-predictions of each component taken by itself. The *practical* problem manifested itself in measurement aberrations from theoretically predicted values when, e.g., three stellar bodies (Earth, Sun, Moon) were involved.

The linearity principle was one conceptual cornerstone for the Newtonian endeavor to see 'everything' in the universe as governed by one corpus of mathematicized natural laws valid across any imaginable scale variation: big-small, slow-fast, few-many … . It was indeed a worrying thought if the linearity principle was to lose its validity already when an aggregate had as few as three components. For such reasons the Swedish King, Oscar II (1929-1907), who was a keen supporter of the arts and sciences, made solution of the three-body problem the objective of a scientific prize competition on the occasion of his 60th birthday. Even if Poincaré didn't deliver the wished-for solution[5], he was awarded the prize in 1889.

The story around Poincaré's publication of his prize-winning paper has become famous in the history of science-literature (the following account is based on Barrow-Green 1996 and Bradley 2006): A few days before his text was to be printed (in the journal *Acta Mathematica*) Poincaré recog-

---

5   The Jury's verdict quoted from Wikipedia / J.H. Poincaré, 16.7.11: *"This work cannot indeed be considered as furnishing the complete solution of the question proposed, but it is nevertheless of such importance that its publication will inaugurate a new era in the history of celestial mechanics."*

nized that it contained a critical error. Correction of the error opened up for completely new perspectives on the problems he had been investigating. The full implications of his discoveries were developed during the following year and published in a new *Acta Mathematica* paper (Poincaré 1890). This paper (in the words of Bradley 2006: 135) proved to become foundational for "chaos theory, the branch of mathematics that studies the orderly patterns that occur in seemingly random situations. In such mathematical systems, small changes in initial conditions can produce significant variations in output".

Unlike Epicurus' atomic swerving concept, the "small changes in initial conditions" that, according to Poincaré's mathematical reasoning, were capable of producing "significant variations in output" were no product of Poincaré's personal imagination or intuition. Standard natural scientific terminology described such "small changes" as part of a *potential energy* pool always present in freely moving mechanical aggregates – partly as a result of past collision- or force-based interactivity amongst aggregate components (or interactivity between aggregate components and aggregate-external forces). Unlike *kinetic energy*, which is responsible for the measurable movement of aggregate components, the additional potential energy pool was known to be there but wasn't attended to in the linear equations used to predict the future movement of the aggregate. Such potential energy was considered an unavoidable background noise that needed not be taken into account, given that it didn't in any measurable way influence the movement of singular aggregate components. Poincaré himself likened this potential energy to minute pendular movements left as traces with singular particles due to their accidental collisions with other particles immediately prior to measurement. The amplitude of these pendular movements was not sufficient to influence particle movement – just as a resonating tuning fork may move forward in a straight line without being measurably affected by the vibrations of its branches. Yet, staying with the tuning fork-analogy we know that its resonance amplitude, as expressed in sound volume, is heightened if it happens to come across another tuning fork with comparable wavelengths. The same applies to the potential energy belonging to aggregate components. Based as they are on earlier encounters with other aggregate components, they get amplified in case their carrier-components happen to make contact with new components with which they are in sync. Whether or not, or with what volume such amplification takes place cannot, however, be predicted with certitude, but only as a matter of probabilities.

Having now sketched the basic findings coming out of Poincaré's investigation of the Three-Body Problem, I shall describe, first, how these findings found their observable counterparts in the real world, and, secondly, what is implied by using a memory metaphor to make (partial) sense of the findings.

Poincaré Resonance and the Memory Metaphor

For more than half a century Poincaré's work remained a purely theoretical contribution to mathematical physics. The advent of computers during the 1960-70s made it possible to simulate the theoretical scenarios imagined by Poincaré.

The so-called *Butterfly Effect* illustrates a computer-based simulation of the way "small changes in initial conditions can produce significant variations in output".

The Butterfly Effect was first registered and named by Edward Lorentz[6]. While working on a computer-supported weather prediction he 'happened to' alter his computational platform from one of six, to one of three decimals – and found that predictions were significantly altered as a consequence. Viewed in a macrophysical perspective the alteration introduced was minimal ('a virtual flapping of a butterfly's wing in Texas'). As it turned out, this minimal alteration had a capacity to amplify itself with the end result of bringing about 'a hurricane in Brazil' – as Lorenz, with metaphorical looseness, put it.

In complexity literature the peculiar snowball quality of phenomena like the Butterfly Effect are described as *the emergence of a novel attractor*: the sudden birth of a movement trajectory that had not, till then, been part of the movement repertoire of a given large-scale aggregate.[7]

Prigogine (1997) pays tribute to Poincaré by calling the potential energy he had studied *Poincaré resonance*. Describing Poincaré resonance as somehow analogous to memory is not my invention. This terminology is

---

6 Lorentz' Butterfly Effect-discovery took place in 1961 and was described in Lorenz 1963.

7 According to Prigogine, 1997, the number of components in aggregates large enough for complexity phenomena to occur exceeds 10^{23}.

broadly used in complexity literature[8] – which is not to be wondered at. Poincaré resonance is a quality that attaches to all sorts of bodies engaged in mutual interaction, ranging from elementary particles to billiard balls to planets. The quality reflects past events in the movement trajectory of one particular body: encounters it has had with other bodies. As long as the body in question is 'just with itself' the resonance it is carrying doesn't show directly: It represents a mere *potential* for action. This potential, however, may become released, and thus become directly observable, in case the body meets other bodies that somehow invite the quality to get amplified and overtly expressed.

In the realm of lifeless matter such an invitation may occasion event sequences akin to the Butterfly Effect. If, in a loose metaphorical way, we apply the above description to the human realm, a scenario like the following may be imagined:[9]

> - *Location*: The City Hall Square of Copenhagen one dark, wintry evening. A person, Anne, is dimly seen, walking along. Another person, Bent, apparently recognizes Anne from behind, approaches her, touches her lightly on the shoulder.
> - *Anne*: Screaming out loud …
> - *Bent*: "What's the matter, it's me, I just touched you … "
> - *Anne*: "Oh my god, you scared the wits out of me. No, I know it wasn't your fault, but I just come from the cinema: My favourite Hitchcock movie, I saw it for the 5th time. I really love it, but, oh my God, it makes me all jittery!"

The described scenario is about one body (embodied person), Anne, who carries memory traces along with her from one encounter, namely with a Hitchcock film, into a new encounter, namely with Bent. The memory traces, which are completely accidental to her relationship with Bent,

---

8   In *The end of Certainty* Prigogine only makes use of the memory-terminology once (1997: 125):"As a result, irreversibility leads to long memory effects that profoundly alter macroscopic physics". But see also the immediately following footnote.

9   In Prigogine (1990: 22) we find this metaphorical comparison between Poincaré resonance and human interactivity: "The formation of correlations is somewhat reminiscent to that of a couple which has a conversation (this would correspond to a collision). Even when the partners go away, the memory of their conversation remains. The information associated to this conversation (…) is spreading out to more and more participants."

attune her in a way that is supposedly different from the attunement she might have carried with her from an encounter with a romantic feel-good movie – or (for that matter) from an announcement from her doctor that she had contracted incurable breast cancer. In semi-technical psychological language the attunement might be described as affective resonance (Parr 2002) or emotional sharing (Singer & Lamm 2009). Concepts like mirror neurons (Rizzolatti & Sinigaglia 2008) or vitality affects (Stern 2010) might be invoked. Had Anne not, then and there, met Bent, her special attunement would have worn off, just as Poincaré resonance in lifeless matter aggregates will do if the carrier-body doesn't run into bodies that may elicit an amplifier effect.

The scenario just presented involved only two persons and a movie screen. Depending on the quality of the Anne-Bent relationship, and also on the attunement Bent happens to bring along to their encounter, the incident need not carry any further consequences.

The following scenario is translated (with editorial changes) from a text I recently wrote on complexity in organizational settings (Willert 2010). Here attunement effects are expanded into emotional contagion (Hatfield et al. 1994), in principle analogous to a Butterfly Effect – now in an organizational setting.

> 'Everybody' has experienced organizations to be alive in the sense that, all of a sudden, some particular mood brings unexpected qualities to evolve in habitual settings:
>
> When *the morning staff meeting* began everybody believed – in the phraseology of Heraclitus – that the river they were going to put their feet in was the same old river they knew from hundreds of other mornings. By the end of this particular morning staff meeting everybody was, if not distinctly wiser, then deeply puzzled. What on earth had triggered those exasperated exchanges, apparently coming out of nowhere, but leading to a harsh reactivation of a conflict that had officially been buried and 'forgotten' more than half a year ago and had never been alluded to since – for the good reason that it represented a lose-lose situation?
>
> "Why had nobody seen it coming? – What is management for, if not to prevent such breaches in organizational self-confidence from happening?" – staff members may have asked themselves.

> But what if the incident was partly triggered by sources external to the organizational set-up? – just like, in the Three-Body Problem, gravitational forces external to the bounded unit of Sun, Moon and Earth make exact movement prediction of these three heavenly bodies impossible.
>
> Let's say twelve persons took part in the said morning staff meeting. Each of the twelve has brought body- and mind-based memory stuff with them from life-worlds being not directly related to the organizational setting: A tear-filled saying good-bye to the three year old at the crèche; a letter received that very morning announcing positive pregnancy test results; a row with the wife; a letter announcing that "we have read your letter of (last week) with great interest and would be pleased to see you for a recruitment interview with our board of directors on (the day after tomorrow) … ". Memory traces (personal attunement) thus carried along by staff meeting participants will *not necessarily* have traceable effects on meeting transactions. They may be kept within the bodily and mental confines of their person-carriers as part of a *potential* energy pool present in any organizational scenario. Memory traces, however, may also attach themselves to, and have effects upon the way scenarios develop. Shit happens (excuse my French – but so it does!). A particular interactivity constellation, involving timing/persons/issues, but *seemingly* coming out of nowhere, *may* trigger an organizational Butterfly Effect like the one observed during this particular morning staff meeting.

My account of the discovery and implications of memory/time-binding effects in the realm of pre-biotic matter has come to an end. I now move on to outline the role of memory in the realm of the biosphere.

Memory in biosphere: supporting actor fitness through trial and error learning

When dealing with non-living/pre-biotic matter our focus was on lifeless bodies and aggregates of such bodies that were acted on by mechanical forces. Such individual, lifeless bodies were seen to 'possess' a kind of memory (Poincaré resonance) reflecting past events. These memory effects, however, had no functional value for the individual bodies as such.

The effects might simply fade away, meaning that the body would lose the potential energy it had briefly 'possessed'. Or the effects might contribute to some amplification processes, e.g. of the Butterfly variety, with possible ramifications far removed from the body that triggered or contributed to the amplification. Whatever the fate of the memory effects, they would in no way alter the lifeless body's way of responding to future events it came across.

This state-of-affairs changes when we move into the realm of the bio-sphere. Here (as the above headline tells us) memory serves the function of *supporting actor fitness through trial and error learning*. To understand how this is brought about we need to look into the terms 'actor', 'fitness' and 'trial and error learning'.

Actors are *living* bodies, or organisms, but organisms vary greatly in the scope and extent of their actor capacity. What characterizes *any* organism is that its existence (survival) depends on the way it manages to feed on its environment by maintaining an energy flow (metabolism) across the boundary line between itself and its surroundings. The organism, or species to which it belongs, is said to be fit (enjoy a measure of fitness) to the extent that organism-environment exchanges secure survival at individual and collective levels. Taken as a whole, the biosphere has produced a huge amount of fitness strategies that have become embodied in the form of species and their organism members. 'Scope and extent of actor capacity' figure as one strategic parameter making one species different from others. Rooted plants may have a high fitness score – but still a very limited action potential if compared to highly evolved animals with a strong locomotive capacity. Generally speaking, the fitness supporting function of memory is positively correlated with the 'size' of a given organism's actor capacity.

In order to outline the ways in which memory shapes biospheric events I shall make a distinction between three temporal frames.

Phylogenesis represents the bio-sphere's most extensive, and indeed all-encompassing temporal frame. Phylogenesis got going more than 3.000 million years ago (Margulis et al. 2011: 1). Phylogenesis may be conceived of as a vast laboratory for producing ecologically viable species, i.e. organismic form endowed with fitness relative to certain environmental conditions. The type of memory on which species production is dependent I call *genetic memory*. Genetic memory resides in DNA-strings making up genomes. Genomes responsible for the build-up of individual species members may be likened to a highly selective memory pool telling stories of phylogenesis as one unbroken, large-scale trial and error learning process: "What kinds of fitness experiments, i.e. attempted matchmaking between organisms and environments have been tried out, and with what results?" Successful matchmaking leads to retention of genome components. When matchmaking fails, genome components are destroyed. Retained components may later be re-used in future phylogenetic experiments. Thus, there is a rough 95% correspondence between the human and the chimpanzee genomes. Both genomes, however, carry genetic traces referring back to phylogenetic beginnings (Damasio 2010).

My second temporal frame concerns the life spans of individual organisms (ontogenesis). The affiliated memory form I call *organismic memory*. Whereas genetic memory used DNA as its vehicle, organismic memory resides in brains, or, more generally, in central nervous system structures. In organisms with highly evolved actor capacity, action is coupled with evaluation of action effects (Damasio 1994). "Did the just completed action sequence lead to positive or negative results as seen in the light of organism-specific value criteria?" Actions leading to positive results tend to become repeated. Those leading to negative results will tend to disappear from the action repertoire available to the organism.

My temporal frame number three refers to programmed, goal-directed exchanges across the organism-environment border. The exchanges may entail interactions between organisms and some lifeless 'partners' (as in eating, or constructing a nest) or with other organisms (as in copulating or fighting or hunting a prey). Whatever the circumstances, the exchanges are programmed: they unfold in accordance with certain design features stipulating admissible versus inadmissible exchange, or action components. They are goal-directed in that they have built-in stop rules defining what situational features (target situations) may bring the exchange to a halt. Such exchanges make up a large part of the action repertoire of animal organisms. The fitness of organisms depends on the extent to which this repertoire matches local environmental condition, namely by enabling the organism to carry on its particular way of living its life.

The exchanges unfold as (inter-)action *sequences*, meaning that they entail time-binding, and thus also memory. Compared to memory forms we've met earlier in this text, however, a new quality is added, namely temporal *bi-directionality*. On the one hand, the organism's earlier learning experiences (memories from the past) may influence its particular way of executing the exchange sequences. When an exchange starts, however, the 'memory' that will guide the acting organism refers not to what has taken place, but to what is about to take place: "What design features must be obeyed? – What kind of target situation(s) are we heading for?" What we find here is forward-oriented time-binding residing in neuronal networks responsible for the unfolding of action sequences belonging to the given organism's basic repertoire. I'll call this type of forward-oriented time-binding *functional foresight*.[10] In the following section on memory in the human realm we shall see how functional foresight becomes transformed into *innovative foresight* that allows humans to partially reshape their own life-worlds, and thus, to some extent, their destiny.

My account of the way memory supports actor fitness in the bio-sphere is coming to an end. Compared to memory effects in lifeless matter, time-binding in the bio-sphere leads to much more stable, long-lasting effects directly affecting the memorizing bodies. This enlarged stability and durability of memory effects is brought about by the embedding of memory functions in material substrates specifically designed for time-binding: DNA strings, central nervous systems and neuronal networks.

When moving on to the importance of memory for shaping human life worlds as we know them, we'll meet language and material object structures as new carriers of (external) memory.

Memory in the human realm: supporting life world innovation through actors' individual and collective self-programming

The advent of humans on our planet introduced a new set of operative principles for biosphere regulation. This is the reason for calling human life worlds a new ontological realm. The novelty goes like this:

Like all their biosphere 'colleagues' human actors feed on their external environments through action programs shaped by some combination of genetics and learning: We eat, we build 'nests', we copulate, we get into fights, and some of us even go hunting. In the context of the human realm I'll call such environmental exchanges *first order acting*. In addition human organisms are endowed with the biologically unique capacity to engage in programmed, goal-directed exchanges *with themselves in their capacity as*

---

10 The exchange logic described corresponds to Mead's (1934) description of *gestural conversation*.

first order actors. This biologically unique capacity I'll call second order acting. I'll illustrate what second order acting is all about through a brief phylogenetic account of *mirroring*.

Apes seem to be able to grasp the logic of mirroring. Monkeys don't. For monkeys, and animals further down the phylogenetic ladder, the figure seen in the mirror is 'somebody else', an intruder. Apes capable of mirroring may need some familiarization time when first presented with a mirror. Once they've got used to the idea, they seem able to enjoy being in the (virtual) company of themselves. Byrne (1995: 115) shows the magnificent picture of a chimpanzee intensely studying the underside of its own tongue helped by a mirror. Till now, the chimp has *used* its tongue as an eating tool, and, at best, *known* it as feeling patterns. But now …:"Oh my God (the chimp's expression seems to convey) – and this is how *it looks*!"

Measured with a human yardstick, mirroring capacity is one among many origins of selfhood. The dividing line between the 'acting I' (the organismic actor) and 'all the rest' (the physical and social environment towards which the actor directs its actions) gets blurred. 'Acting I' is not only in here. It has a potential double out there: a body like other bodies – but then also *my* body: 'me'.[11] The tongue-studying chimpanzee is learning new things *about itself*. Its active exploration of *its own* tongue is placed midway between first and second order acting.

Humans have taken mirroring capacity one large step further. As a species, we spend much time, energy and money, not only on observing ourselves from the outside (mirrors, cameras), but also on actively improving our looks (clothes, cosmetics, jewelry, sunbathing). Our bodily outsides become targets for goal-directed action programs.

In addition – and this is where true second order acting comes in – we are genetically equipped to take an actor's attitude towards *our own bodily insides*: our intentions, emotional states, thoughts. We sense or feel and may talk about these inner states as objects in their own right. We spend time, energy and money on improving them, as best we can, in case we find them unsatisfactory, i. e. inadequate as tools for being the actors we want to be. My own professional training is that of a psychologist. As a practitioner I've assisted fellow human beings in

---

11 The distinction I make between 'acting I' and 'me' corresponds in principle to Mead's (1934) I/me distinction.

partly reshaping themselves into (what they thought would be) better versions of themselves-as-actors. Clients and I have patiently collaborated with a view to changing or modifying intentions, emotional states or thoughts which, partly as a result of trial and error learning, had become installed in the clients' lives, but were, nevertheless, experienced by their owners as burdensome.

Thus, apart from being genetically programmed, and being to some extent reprogrammed through learning (as is the case for all subhuman actor organisms), humans are further endowed with a species-specific aptitude to partly reprogram themselves. I shall now discuss some implications following from this aptitude – including the way in which (cf. this section's headline) memory supports human life world *innovation*. First I'll talk about the transformation of functional foresight (as found in subhuman actor organisms) into innovative foresight (as found in humans). Then follows a discussion concerning language as a vehicle for individual and collective human memory.

From functional foresight to innovative foresight

In the above section on *Memory in Biosphere* I pointed out that animals, apart from having their life-courses influenced by stored memories coming from their past, also made use of *functional foresight* when monitoring their programmed, goal-directed exchanges with the external environment. The neural networks responsible for the implementation of such exchanges somehow 'know about' the end-points or target situations which the exchanges are meant to bring about.

In humans, functional foresight is found in two varieties. One variety – corresponding in principle to what is found in the rest of the animal kingdom – may be described as habit driven. Habit driven foresight guides the organism in accordance with *what has worked before*. The other variety I call innovative foresight. Humans may generate ideas about target situations that do not match anything they have, so far, encountered, but which they would, nevertheless, *wish to see realized*, yet without, as yet, knowing how such a realization might be brought about. Before ground breaking cultural innovations like steam engines, atomic bombs and moon rockets existed as real world objects they existed as mental images – together with ideas about action sequences that might *make* them real. And real they did become. Innovative foresight is one prerequisite for such a feat.

As stated above, the human capacity for engaging in *linguistic* exchange processes with oneself and others is yet another functional prerequisite for innovative life world construction.

Human language as a vehicle for externalized individual and collective human memory

Even when successful, the action sequences taking a person from innovative foresight to full realization of what was foresighted may be a long one. The mental images guiding the process must be remembered and/or adjusted from beginning till end. Mental images may be very vivid when experienced – but they are also fleeting. When mental images are described in language, their cognitive contents are more easily remembered – not only by the describing person, but also by those listening in his social surroundings. The cognitive contents of the images become shared and thus the property, not only of the original image owner, but also of the community to which she belongs.

Such language-based exchange processes have been part and parcel of human community building since prehistoric times. For a long stretch of time, language was restricted to sound exchanges between persons being within hearing range of each other. When humans, at a certain point in history, started, not just to *talk* language, but also to *write* language, and, later, even to *print* language and to *distribute* printed language as happened after Gutenberg – the importance of language as a vehicle for externalized, and thus jointly accessible, individual and collective human memory escalated enormously (see also Donald 1991). Today, digitalized language (computers, the internet etc.) is taking this escalation even further.

The described historical tendencies bear witness to a generalized movement towards objectification of memory. Not only words in books or on screens guide us in our continued translation of past experiences into present-moment activities which push us into a future. The same holds for all sorts of cultural objects encountered in our human habitat: the houses ('nests') we live in, the technology we use for fighting … yes, and steam engines, atomic bombs, moon rockets. They all tell us stories about where we come from, what and who we are right now, where we may be heading – as individuals, as a species.

Summing up

In this article I've pointed at memory – in a variety of forms – as a bridge building device across the ontological realms of non-living matter, biosphere and human realm. First I dealt with the reality shaping – and complexity generating – effects of memory in non-living matter. My account of memory in biosphere and human realm became unreasonably short. Yet I offered glimpses of the ways in which innovative foresight, conceived as *forward oriented, creative memory*, supplemented by language as a vehicle for *external, shared memory* pave the way for the unique capacity of the human species to partially reshape reality on a vast scale. Innovative foresight allows humans to create virtual scenarios that may be fairly improbable in and of themselves – but, still, realizable in so far as human actors decide to try out the virtual action plans that are attached to the scenarios.[12] Not only are we reprogramming ourselves. By reprogramming ourselves we become re-programmers of our external environment (steam engines, atomic bombs, moon rockets …) – and have to find ways of coping with the consequences.

This way of describing mankind's unique position in world affairs allows me to, briefly, return to the theme of determinism/free will which, as stated in the introduction, motivated, first Epicurus, then, 2.200 years later, Prigogine to promote the complexity viewpoint. Epicurus and Prigogine both saw determinism as a mental straitjacket. Both believed that the potential efficacy of human will power might be salvaged by conceiving of world evolution as being governed by some mix of linearity-based, Parmenidean predictability and random, i.e. unpredictable, Heraclitic fluctuation. Were they right? Does complexity leave room for understanding human willing as one among a number of his-

---

12 George Herbert Mead (1934: 6) was giving much attention to (as he called it) the *natural teleology* inherent in animal activity, including its human variety. Today, cognitive neuroscientists are busy documenting functional and location-based similarities between backward-/forward-oriented 'memory' (Atance & O'Neill 2001; Botzung et al. 2008; Addis et al. 2007).

tory-shaping forces rather than viewing it as one among mankind's self-comforting, but scientifically unfounded illusions?[13]

I believe it does – but in a highly qualified sense.

Free will may be discussed as an issue concerning man's ability to accomplish *what she wants*: This discussion frame makes freedom dependent on the capacity of human actions to, actually, reach their intended target situations. By describing the world as partly governed by unpredictability, complexity theory repudiates the generalized possibility of such a capacity. Yet, had it not been for humans using innovative foresight (and language) as a vehicle for their willing, the current human habitat 'peopled' by houses, fighting utensils (atomic bombs included), steam engines, moon rockets ... – and all the rest – would not exist. This is a brute historical fact that must be acknowledged and taken into account no matter how human willing and freedom are conceptualized.

Below I'll present my personal conceptualizations of willing and freedom as these have been molded by the ideas presented in this article on *The Natural History of Memory*.

Classical science promoted the idea of predetermined linear order as *definitely* governing all observable movement in lifeless matter, and *probably* also governing what went on in the animal world and in human life worlds. Whether counter-intuitive or not, necessity in the guise of determinism was king. The complexity viewpoint dethrones necessity as king. Necessity and freedom are always entwined. Energy forms, the nature of which may in principle become known, are *continually* forcing the observable movements of material objects, animals and humans into predictable patterns. At the same time material objects, animals and humans are thus constituted, and thus linked to their surroundings, that predictability may *at any time*, and *in any place* break down. Breakdown of predictability may be understood as the kind of freedom bestowed upon the world by complexity. Material objects are free to relate themselves to objects with which they resonate in sync possibly starting a butterfly effect of sorts. Animals are free to flee from a situation which, in a here and now perspective, looks appealing – because their memory reminds them they got beaten up during their last encounter with that same situation.

---

13 History-of-science literature often refer to Newton, Darwin and Freud as the trio shattering Western man's illusions concerning personal or collective willing as a tool for controlling world affairs. Daniel Wegner (2002) is a present-day experimental psychologist trying to prove them right.

Humans are free to desist from doing what, as first order actors, they are normally doing.[14] As secondary actors they are also free to engage in planning preferred action alternatives – even action alternatives which, in a world-wide perspective, represent *absolute novelty*. The first steam engine built was truly *the first* of its kind. Human freedom, however, does not extend to knowing what will be the large-scale results (target situations) towards which our shared action repertoire is leading us.

---

14 Benjamin Libet (e.g. Libet et al. 1999) is an experimental psychologist whose research started a movement towards making operational sense out of the concepts of willing and freedom.

References

Barrow-Green, J. 1996, *Poincaré and the three body Problem*, Providence (RI): American Mathematical Society.

Bradley, M.J. 2006, *The Foundations of Mathematics, 1800-1900*, New York: Chelsea House.

Byrne, R. 1995, *The Thinking Ape*, Oxford: Oxford University Press.

Damasio, A. 1994, *Descartes' Error*, New York: Putnam.

Damasio, A. 2010, *Self Comes to Mind*, London: Heinemann.

Deacon, T.W. 2012, *Incomplete Nature. How Mind emerged from Matter*. New York: W.W. Norton.

Donald, M. 1991, *Origins of the Modern Mind*, Cambridge (Mass.): Harvard University Press.

Gregersen, N.H., ed. 2003, *From Complexity to Life. On the Emergence of Life and Meaning*, Oxford: Oxford University Press.

Griffin, D. 2002, *The Emergence of Leadership*, New York: Routledge.

Hatfield, E., Cacioppo, J.T., Rapson, R.L. 1994, *Emotional Contagion*, Cambridge (UK): Cambridge University Press.

Libet, B., Freeman, A. & Sutherland, K., eds. 1999, *The Volitional Brain*, Thorverton (UK): Imprint Academic.

Lorenz, E.N. 1963. Deterministic Nonperiodic Flow. *Journal of the Atmospheric Sciences,* 20 (2): 130-141.

Margulis, L., Asikainen, C.A. & Krumbein, W.E., eds. 2011, *Chimeras and Consciousness. Evolution of the Sensory Self*, Cambridge (Mass.): MIT Press.

Marion, R. 1999, *The edge of Organization*, Thousand Oaks (Calif.): Sage Publications.

Mead, G.H. 1934, *Mind, Self and Society*, Chicago: Chicago University Press.

O'Keefe, T. 2005, *Epicurus on Freedom*, Cambridge: Cambridge University Press.

Parr, L. 2002, Understanding Others' Emotions: From Affective resonance to empathic Action. In: *Brain & Behavioral Sciences, vol 25*: 44-45.

Poincaré, J. H. 1890, Sur le problème des trois corps et les équations de la dynamiqe. *Acta Mathematica, 13,* 1-270.

Prigogine, I. 1997, *The End of Certainty. Time, Chaos and the New Laws of Nature*, New York: The Free Press.

Prigogine, I. 2002, *Dynamics of correlations for integrable and non-integrable systems: A two levels formulation of laws of nature.* CERN Lecture on Science and Society, Cern, Geneva, Jan. 24, 2002 (DVD).

Prigogine, I. 2003, *Is Future Given?* New Jersey: World Scientific Publishing Company.

Rizzolatti, G., Sinigaglia, C. 2008, *Mirrors in the Brain. How We Share our Actions and Emotions*, Oxford: Oxford University Press.

Shaw, P. 2002, *Changing Conversations in organizations*, New York: Routledge.

Singer, T & Lamm, L. 2009, The Social Neuroscience of Empathy. *Annals of the New York Academic Sciences, vol. 1156: 81-96.*

Stacey, R. 2007, *Strategic Management and organizations Dynamics. 5th Ed.* New York: Prentice Hall.

Stern, D. 2010, *Forms of Vitality: Exploring Dynamic Experience in Psychology and the Arts*, Oxford: Oxford University Press

Søholm, T. & Willert, S., eds. 2010. *Action Learning Consulting.* Copenhagen: Dansk Psykologisk Forlag.

Wegner, D. M. 2002, *The Illusion of Conscious Will*, Cambridge (Mass.): MIT Press.

Tina Maria Fussenegger

From Static Cultures to Complex Societies
Complexity as an Ideological Tool of Description and Assessment

Within Social Anthropology complexity is seen as a development, a goal of evolution, something, which never stands still. Because of its inherent characteristics to develop and evolve, although the term is often defined within momentary descriptions of societies or cultures, complexity mostly implies everlasting movement.

There seems to be a contemporary truth which describes the world as becoming more and more complex. This "truth", partly originating from findings within the field of social evolutionism (Barnard 2003: 62) is problematic, because of the complexity implied while using the term "world". Trying to explain the complexity of a world, which yet has to be defined, is as useless for social anthropology as it should be for other sciences, if the point of view is not clarified.

The aim of this essay is therefore to introduce some of the different points of view, which have contributed to the definitions and clarification processes of complexity. In order to show how the term and the concept was applied and also used, central findings and ideas of social anthropology will be presented, some by contrasting them to exemplary more and less recent paradigms, which played or still play an important role within this field of science.

Cultural and Social Evolution within Social Anthropology

The concept of the cultural and social evolution of the human species has dominated social sciences and social anthropology since the late nineteenth century. It fought a lost battle trying to maintain what was left, while other paradigms, which focused for instance on reflexivity and relativity, came central to the discipline.

> "The concept [cultural evolution] lost currency in cultural anthropology by the end of the twentieth century, when ideas of history and reflexivity came to dominate theoretical discourses." (McGuire 2006: 185)

In the twentieth century the controversies between the different schools reached a peak, which is mirrored by articles published in the American Anthropologist.

> "[I]f Boas and his school rejected the developmental schemes of Tylor and Morgan this must, in no sense, be ascribed to the inadequacies and crudities of those schemes, but rather to the fact they rejected all developmental sequences. [...] Boas always took a prevailingly antagonistic position." (Radin 1939: 303, cited in White 1947: 403-404)

Developmental sequences are central to the notion of cultural evolution, as societies or entities are believed to go through different stages of development to reach a certain ultimate goal of evolution, which culminated in a complex but ordered society (see Barnard 2003: 62).

One of the most important representatives of social or cultural evolution and anthropologist is Herbert Spencer. He introduced the concept of evolution into the scientific community and made it generally known (Carneiro 1973: 77). His definition of "evolution" is as follows:

> "In the original edition of First Principles (1862), Spencer [...] had defined evolution as 'a change from an indefinite, incoherent homogeneity, to a definite, coherent heterogeneity; through continuous differentiations and integrations.' In later editions he modified this definition, further characterizing evolution

as 'an integration of matter and concomitant dissipation of motion' (1896: 407).." (Spencer 1863: 216, cited in Carneiro 1973: 77-78)

The phrasing "incoherent homogeneity" as contrasted to "coherent heterogeneity" implies chaos versus order and simplicity versus … what? Complexity? Difficulty? Artfullness? Although Spencer speaks of an "increase in complexity of structure and function" (Spencer 1973: 461-462, cited in Carneiro 1973: 93) the immediate antonym of "simplicity" is not quite clear. But as the goal of evolution is rather unclearly defined as an increase of complexity (see above), apparent in the development of "human culture […] from very simple beginnings in to large, complex systems" (Glaessen 2005: 213), complexity is linked to intelligence and fertility:

> "Mind cells and sex cells compete for the same materials. Excess of fertility stimulates greater mental activity because the more people there are, the more ingenuity is required to stay alive. The least intelligent individuals and races die off, and the level of intelligence gradually rises." (Harris 2001:127)

In relation to this view, Spencer makes another distinction, namely between different kinds of societies. Spencer distinguishes between "militant" and "industrial" societies and attributes "voluntary cooperation" and "peaceful exchange" to the latter, whereas militant societies are based on compulsory cooperation (Long 2004: 25). In an advanced society, where peace and intelligence rule, militancy is not necessary.

This view of society is greatly problematic, because it is based on the notion of the inferiority of mind of certain groups of people, which he deduces from hereditary intrinsic factors:

> "In his Principles of Sociology (1879), Spencer divided the causes of what he called superorganic phenomena into 'original extrinsic' and 'original intrinsic' factors. The latter consist of the physical, emotional, and intellectual traits characteristic of the individual members of a given group. Taken together, these intrinsic traits defined what Spencer frequently called 'the nature of the social units', that is, the hereditary disposition of the indi-

viduals in the group. The intrinsic factors interacted with the extrinsic factors – organic and in organic conditions – to bring about sociocultural evolution." (Harris 2001: 130)

Defining characteristical traits within certain societies is based on the notion that an entity of people is a bounded and closed group, although a "continuous differentiation and interpretation [of knowledge?]" takes place. This complexity, which states ethnic belonging and culture as interdependent, is a "complexity within". This point of view enables the notion that in the "race to the top, many societies had been left behind" (Glaessen 2005: 213).

Extrinsic factors allowed a certain amount of new input into societies in order to stimulate change, but the relationships between different groups of people where not seen as a central source for development and change. In evolutionist thinking societies therefore mostly generate themselves, taking in to account only few extrinsic factors.

Describing Change with Ethnicity

As mentioned before, cultural and social evolution is a broadly contested concept within social anthropology. Because of the later widely declined notion of developmental sequences and bounded groups, new ways to cope with complexity emerged. As the concept of complexity or describing complexity never stands alone, there are always other heuristic instruments and concepts related to it. A central one in social anthropology is "ethnicity".

Fredrik Barth, a Norwegian social anthropologist, editor of "Ethnic Groups and Boundaries" (1969), an essay collection where a group of social anthropologists including him, published revolutionary thoughts on how to deal with ethnicity, states as follows:

> "Most anthropologists at the time [in the 60s, 70s] thought, at least implicitly, that the world could be described usefully as a discontinuous array of entities called societies, each with its internally shared culture, and that this framed the issues of ethnicity." (Barth 1998: 5)

While criticising a long-held perception on the development of societies, he reintroduces and reinvents the concept "ethnicity". In the words of Barth:

> "[...] ethnicity is a matter of social organization above and beyond questions of empirical cultural differences: it is about 'the social organization of culture difference'". Further on he remarks "that ethnic identity is a matter of self-ascription and ascription by others in interaction, not the analyst's construct on the basis of his or her construction of a group's 'culture' [...]" (Barth 1998: 6).

The re-evaluation of "ethnic distinctions" leads to them as now being recognised as potential instruments of describing change, because they manifest in "social interaction" and are "often the very foundation" from which societies emerge (Barth 1998: 10). Taking into account the interconnectedness of ethnicities and social interaction as a means to describe change, Barth states:

> "Without being able to specify the boundaries of cultures, it is not possible to construct phyletic lines in the more rigorous evolutionary sense. But from the analysis that has been argued here, it should be possible to do so for ethnic groups, and thus in a sense for those aspects of culture which have this organizational anchoring." (Barth 1998: 38)

Barth reinvents ethnicity in a way which allows him to maintain a historical perspective and at the same time getting rid of the possible notion of bounded and independent groups. His concept is open, but yet founded on a methodological and theoretical basis.

The focus on complexity lies therefore within the interconnectedness of social interactions between groups. This "In-Between" complexity centres more on the description of processes and by doing so, structures are considered as well.

Before examining two of the contemporary theories, which deal with change and complexity in the world (Arjun Appadurai and George E. Marcus), German-speaking departments of social anthropology will be presented with respect to their profile exhibited on their Websites. By doing so, contemporary trends in the science field are identified. Also, the possible presence or absence of the concept "complexity" will highlight or devalue a claim to occupy oneself with the mentioned topic.

Social Anthropology Today

If you check websites of German-speaking departments of cultural and social anthropology, the descriptions of the subject matters are quite similar.

Modern Social Anthropology complexity is defined within processes and not structures, as stated on the Website of Cultural and Social Anthropology of the University of Frankfurt:

> "As the constitution and classification of anthropological topics is getting more and more problematic, the scientific interests switch from structures to processes. Cultures are less seen as static, long-lasting systems of norms, values and opinions but as fields of discourse, where norms, values and interpretations are being negotiated/contested, where interpretations are being created and disintegrated and where institutions and ideas from 'the outside' are transferred into the own system and developed creatively." (Fakultät für Kulturwissenschaften, Vergleichende Kultur- und Sozialanthropologie, Frankfurt, translated from German)

Whereas the University of Frankfurt mentions a change in the subject of Social Anthropology, the University of Marburg focuses more on the ability to investigate different contexts.

> "Cultural and Social Anthropology in Marburg emphasizes on the mediation of actual international expert knowledge. The ability to investigate empirically and self-reliantly and to analyse theoretically processes of transformation, their causes, dynamics and consequences in local, regional, national and transnational contexts is central to the professional training and research activities of the area of expertise." (Kultur- und Sozialanthropologie, Philipps Universität Marburg, 28.01.2012; translated from German)

The University of Berlin even claims that Social Anthropology plays a chief part in the understanding of the "complex present":

> "Given the increasing globalised world, where local, national and global processes are interwoven, the 'science of the culturally different' plays a chief part for the understanding of the complex presence. [...] in the context of global and transnational linkages in the synopsis of micro- and macro-levels." (Freie Universität Berlin, Institut für Ethnologie, Berlin, translated from German)

When complexity is termed, it is within a context of interactions between local, national and global processes. The "simple" investigation of local and more secluded societies has not been pointed out. The Institute of Cultural and Social Anthropology of the University of Vienna mentions the change in the scientific approach of the subject and also refers to the now non-relevant occupation with "simply organised and structured societies":

"In the past the attention of the discipline was drawn to simply organised and structured societies beyond the industrialised world. Today mostly processes linked to colonialism, globalisation and the worldwide flows of migration are focused upon. At the same time conventional topics like local-cultural interaction, forms of organisation and worldviews are being enhanced and the intensive fieldwork while applying the method of 'participating observation' remains a defining characteristic of the discipline." (Universität Wien, Institut für Kultur- und Sozialanthropologie, translated from German)

Although not every German-speaking University uses the term "complexity" specifically in their statements, they all refer to it in some way ("local, national and global processes are interwoven", "understanding of the complex present", etc.). Also it seems that the notion of processes involves a greater complexity and authorised scientific approach than the notion of structures (see above).

Reading the last statement of the Department of Social and Cultural Anthropology in Vienna, it appears that this one is the most neutral in relation to their personal power to influence the contemporary subject matter. They state what is being done and therefore at the same time what the work of their department focuses upon. The mention of "worldwide flows" (although only mentioned in relation to migration) is interesting, as we have a focal point on the global perspective and also a reference to one of the very widely debated contemporary theories of global change, namely by Arjun Appadurai. His and George E. Marcus' insights are those which the following chapter centres on.

Modern Theories – The World as a Complex Place?

The human world can be imagined as a place, where every action someone takes will influence the life of someone else. This general idea is taken on by many contemporary theories, based on the notion of the interconnectedness of people, which Anthropologist Eric Wolf emphasizes in his book "Europe and the People Without History" (1982).

> "The idea was to show that human societies and cultures would not be properly understood until we learned to visualize them in their mutual interrelationships and interdependencies in space and time." (Wolf 1997: X)

The demands of such an approach are nearly impossible. It is highly complicated to put human society *and* culture into a relative perspective towards space and time, taking into account their interconnectedness, without thinking of further foundations of human existence. One powerful way of thinking, but limited with regard to "time", is the point of view Arjun Appadurai suggests.

Arjun Appadurai is a Social Anthropologist, born in Bombay and now teaching in New York. In one of his books "Modernity At Large: Cultural Dimensions of Globalization" (1996) he talks about global cultural economy and the order of things in the globalised world, which is overlapping and disjunctive. Because of this, center-periphery-models don't work anymore. The model he proposes, concentrates on disjunctions, which are framed by five dimensions within the cultural-global flow: ethnoscapes, mediascapes, technoscapes, financescapes and ideoscapes. He talks of flows, because wherever you stand as an actor in the global picture, the perspective is constructed differentially. Appadurai calls them "'imagined worlds', that is, the multiple worlds which are constituted by the historically situated imaginations of persons and groups spread around the globe" (Appadurai, cited in Kreff 2003: 132). The five flows are thus described as followed:

- **Ethnoscapes**: are real and imagined movements, which influence stabilities everywhere. The term "ethnoscapes" should substitute earlier concepts which focus on entities, like village, society or locality.
- **Technoscapes**: describe the global flow marked by the configuration of technology, which often ignores boundaries and depends on the flow of money, political circumstances and the availability of work.
- **Financescapes**: illustrate the worldwide flow of global capital, which is difficult to pursue.
- **Ideoscapes**: exhibit ideologies like state-ideologies and their counter ideologies. One can imagine them as interlinking and worldwide available images which are expressed by ideas like "freedom", "rights", "independence" or "democracy". Because they are interpreted and worked with differently everywhere, their inner coherency is not stable. Different interpretations of meaning develops.
- **Mediascapes**: constitute of pictures, narrations et cetera ... Electronic devices influence the circulation of knowledge and information. Imagined worlds are constructed, which often have little in common with "real worlds", because they describe the "other" and their possible lives. (Appadurai cited in Kreff 2003: 132-133).

We find ourselves in a situation of deterritorialization and transnational movements. Everything depends on something else, is embedded in a certain context. Appadurai himself declares: "[how] are we to compare fractally shaped cultural forms that are also polythetically overlapping in their coverage of terrestrial space?" (Appadurai 1996: 46, cited in Kreff 2003: 138) His proposal is to look for a human theory of chaos, which focuses on the dynamic of the constitution of the world and not on stable systems (ibid.). Therefore the theory and methodology of research in social anthropology has to be adapted to the current situation in the world. One of the problems he outlines regarding adaptation, is the "relationship [...] between place, comparison, and generalization" (Appadurai 1986: 359):

> "Where comparison (and generalization) have been successful in anthropology, they have occurred most often in the context of small-scale societies and have involved highly schematized aspects of social life, such as kinship terminology. As the societies under consideration become more complex, literate, and histori-

cal, the kind of decontextualization that facilitates generalization becomes harder to accomplish." (Appadurai 1986: 359)

Appadurai takes it as a fact, that societies are becoming more complex, which allows him to draw the conclusion that a rightful generalising of research results is more unlikely to achieve. In relation to research topics he finds anthropological work concerning complex societies lacking in variety, because he criticizes the gridlocked connection between certain societies and issues. "[S]imple theoretical handles become metonyms and surrogates for the civilization or society as a whole: hierarchy in India, [...]." (Appadurai 1986: 357) The question, how complexity in societies within a global context can be taken into account, while researching issues at hand, is not fully answered by him, although the framework of his theories is highly inspiring (see Albrow 1998: 1411-1412).

Whereas Appadurai concentrates on the global rather than on the local, and more on space than on time, George E. Marcus offers a differentiated way of dealing with complexity between world-system, global and local. According to him "multi-sited ethnography" could offer a solution for the current theoretical and methodological problems at hand. He defines it as follows:

> "Ethnography moves from its conventional single-site location, contextualized by macro-constructions of a larger social order, such as the capitalist world system, to multiple sites of observation and participation that cross-cut dichotomies such as the 'local' and the 'global', the 'lifeworld' and the 'system'" (Marcus 1995: 95, cited in Kreff 2003: 170).

Marcus' aim is to overcome the global/local dichotomy by integrating the global within the local. He claims that if you do ethnography of cultural arrangements within the world-system, at the same time you have an ethnography of the system itself. The global is the newly arising dimension of antagonism by connecting localities in the context of multi-sited ethnography (Kreff 2003: 170-171).

According to Marcus there are three major points to consider, when developing such ethnography. First there is contemporaneity: It is important to show how actions, which occur at the same time within interlaced contexts, influence each other. Second, we need a comparing dimension which allows us to contrast localities to each other, independent of their interlacing nature. Third, ethnography searches for that which, apart from the public dominant, stands out of discourse and action (ibid.).

The aim of representing and describing different sites in the world in this way is not "holistic":

> "[M]ulti-sited ethnography [...] claims that any ethnography of a cultural formation in the world system is also an ethnography of the system, and therefore cannot be understood only in terms of the conceptional single-site mise-en-scene of ethnographic research, assuming indeed it is the cultural formation, produced in several different locals, rather than the conditions of a particular set of subjects that is the object of study. For ethnography, then, there is no global in the local-global contrast now so frequently evoked. The global is an emergent dimension of arguing about the connection among sites in a multi-sited ethnography." (Marcus 1995: 99)

When post-modern theory displays complexity within global processes, which are consistently reproduced and contested in different ways from different standpoints, the possibility of comparison of, for instance, social evolutionary theories with contemporary ones, doesn't exist any more. The focus of complexity shifted from societies (complexity within) to complexity between or in-between. Although working with a comparative historical angle is becoming more and more difficult, at least the end-time scenario of an ever-growing complexity to a certain end, as for example Herbert Spencer feared it, is more unlikely.

> "If Evolution of every kind is an increase in complexity of structure and function that is incidental to the universal process of equilibration, and if equilibration must end in complete rest, what is the fate towards which all things tend?" (Spencer 1937: 461, cited in Carneiro 1973: 93)

If switching from one point of view to another makes it more plausible for humanity to survive and develop one might gladly chose survival.

Final Remarks

Terminology is often about trying to change research problems by renaming concepts. But, in many cases, because of a historical perspective, concepts and ideas might be redefined and renamed. As people, societies and therefore the world changes, concepts change with them. For instance, the meaning of complexity in the eighteenth and nineteenth century differs from the meaning and use, complexity has nowadays. Or maybe, as the global perspective within social anthropology is more dominant than two hundred years ago, one could separate or add meanings. For example, speaking of densified societies, communities or flows allows a more concrete image, as complexity as a term is often used to describe the non-explainable. As a scientist the line between "complicated" and "complex" is a fine one.

References

Appadurai, Arjun 1986, *Theory in Anthropology: Center and Periphery*. Comparative Studies in Society and History, Vol. 28, No. 2 (Apr., 1986), pp. 356-361, Cambridge: Cambridge University Press. Stable URL: www.jstor.org/stable/178976.

Albrow, Martin 1998, Review: Modernity at Large: Cultural Dimensions of Globalization by Arjun Appadurai. American Journal of Sociology, Vol. 103, No. 5 (March 1998), pp. 1411-1412. The University of Chicago Press. Stable URL: www.jstor.org/stable/10.1086/231357.

Barnard, Alan 2003, *History and Theory in Anthropology*. Cambridge: Cambridge University Press.

Barth, Fredrik 1998, *Ethnic Groups and Boundaries: The Social Organization of Cultural Difference*. Long Grove, Illinois: Waveland Press, INC.

Carneiro, Robert L. 1973, Structure, Function, and Equilibrium in the Evolutionism of Herbert Spencer. Journal of Anthropological Research, Vol. 29, No. 2 (Summer, 1973), pp. 77-95. University of New Mexico. Stable URL: www.jstor.org/stable/3629984. Carneiro, Robert L. 1986, On the Relationship between Size of Population and Complexity of Social Organisation. Journal of Anthropological Research, Vol. 42, No. 3, Approaches to Culture and Society (Autumn, 1986), pp. 355-364; University of Mexico; Stable URL: www.jstor.org/stable/3630039.

Europa-Universität Viadrina (12.10.2011), Professur für Vergleichende Kultur- und Sozialanthropologie; Fakultät für Kulturwissenschaften, Frankfurt; www.kuwi.euv-frankfurt-o.de/de/lehrstuhl/vs/anthro/index.html.

Freie Universität Berlin (22.12.2011), Institut für Ethnologie Berlin; www.polsoz.fu-berlin.de/ethnologie/studium/master_ska/qualifikation_inhalte/index.html.

Glaessen, Henri J.M. 2005: In: Barnard, Alan/Spencer, Jonathan 2005, Evolution and Evolutionism. In: Encyclopedia of Social and Cultural Anthropology. Routledge, Taylor & Francis Group, London and New York; pp. 213-217.

Harris, Marvin 2001, *The Rise of Anthropological Theory: A History of Theories of Culture*. Updated Edition with an Introduction by Maxine L. Margolis, Walnut Creek, Lanham, New York, Oxford: Altamira Press, A Division of Rowman & Littlefield Publishers, INC.

Kreff, Fernand 2003, *Grundkonzepte der Sozial- und Kulturanthropologie in der Globalisierungsdebatte*, Berlin: Dietrich Reimer Verlag GmbH.

Long, Roderick T. 2004, Herbert Spencer: Libertarian Prophet. In: THE FREEMAN – Ideas On Liberty, July/August 2004; http://praxeology.net/herbertspencerlibertarianprophet.pdf.

Marcus, George E. 1995, Ethnography in/of the World System: The Emergence of Multi-Sited Ethnography. Annual Review of Anthropology, Vol. 24 (1995), pp. 95-117. Annual Reviews. Stable URL: www.jstor.org/stable/2155931.

McGuire, Randall H. 2006, Evolutionism in Cultural Anthropology: A Critical History by Robert L. Carniero. American Antiquity, Vol. 71, No. 1 (Jan., 2006), pp. 185-186. Society for American Archaeology. Stable URL: www.jstor.org/stable/40035328.

Philipps Universität Marburg (28.01.2012), Kultur- und Sozialanthropologie; www.uni-marburg.de/fb03/ivk/vk.

Universität Wien (28.01.2012), Institut für Kultur- und Sozialanthropologie; www.univie.ac.at/ksa/html/inh/inst/inst.htm.

White, Leslie A. 1947, Evolutionism in Cultural Anthropology. American Anthropologist, New Series, Vol. 49, No. 3 (Jul. - Sep., 1947), pp. 400-413. Blackwell Publishing on behalf of the American Anthropological Association. Stable URL: www.jstor.org/stable/663499.

Wolf, Eric R. 1997, *Europe and the People without History*. Berkeley, Los Angeles, London: University of California Press.

Jörg Zeller

The complex logic of social work

The detection of the complexity of the world presupposes an organ that itself is sufficient complex to detect complexity. A thermostat is also an organ or instrument that in a way "detects" how the world proceeds. However, a thermostat isn't complex enough to detect the complexity in this proceeding. I will call an organ being sufficient complex to detect the complexity of the world and its own detection a consciousness. I'm aware that the word 'consciousness' as the English translation of the German 'Bewusstsein' not adequately captures the 'topos' or semantic field surrounding the concept of 'being conscious' in the German version – namely as a combination of consciousness as a very special kind of being and Being itself, understood as epitome of everything existing; or in other words as the world of existing things, states or on-going events.

As I understand it, also the concept of existence doesn't stand autonomous and isolated in a semantic vacuum. The existing understood as the actual being or happening in space-time is conceptually surrounded of and embedded in a universe of possibilities. The actual is soaked with possibilities or in other words the real is the contingent (hic et nunc) result of a universe of alternatives. As a consequence, reality[1] – the world of existing things and happening events – is in a constant state of flux.

---

1   I agree in principle with Nørreklit's 2004 differentiation between 'world' as totality of facts and 'reality' as totality of facts, possibilities, meanings, and values. The (factual) world becomes on this background an abstraction – constructing a totality of beings by ignoring everything and everyone that is a conscious-being or is result of the acting of conscious-beings. Sometimes, however, I allow myself to

Back to consciousness - I know this is an incomprehensible notion – probably because of the complexity of the relation between being conscious and being simpliciter. I don't want, however, to explore this incomprehensiveness here but instead ignore it and pretend to understand consciousness as if there were no questions left how it is able to detect and react to the complexity of the world and its own detection. Furthermore – letting the cat at once out of the bag – from now on I will not only talk about human consciousness as individualized consciousness of a single human being, let's call him *A*, and another conscious single human being, let's call her *B*, but also of a socialized or common human consciousness, let's call it *C*.

This common consciousness is not incorporated in a single human body understood as an anatomical-physiological consciousness organ but *between* a multiplicity of such consciousness organs or consciousness bearers that are anchored in the physic-chemical-biological happening of the world. I will also ignore here the incomprehensiveness of the notions 'consciousness-organ' and 'consciousness-bearer'. I pretend to be unproblematic about the fact that consciousness can be borne by human or animal bodies. It is on the other hand essential for my intentions in this article that consciousness can't walk around disembodied. It is part of the basic constitution of consciousness that it is psycho-physically and in the human standard case even socio-psycho-physically anchored in a physic-chemical-biological reality enriched by human artifacts.

To adumbrate the complexity of my exemplary conscious beings, *A*, *B*, and *C*, so is it clear that the former two not only have a human body but for instance also a gender – with all its anatomic, physiological and socio-psychological consequences. *C* in its part is in its way to conceptualize and interact with reality affected by the sexuality of the male and female way of being conscious. Sexuality is inter alia an essential factor in the overall value system of a society. The quest for a good life is usually also the quest for a good sexual partner dealing one's values and ideas of good life. Of course, also sexuality and sexual values have their incomprehensibilities oscillating between the social, mental and biological aspects of gender. And I don't want to dig into this here either.

---

ignore the difference between world and reality and to speak – as if it was possible - "objectively" about reality.

The cultural things and institutions, which C - beyond the human and animal consciousness-bearers and all the other unconscious things - consists of, affect the existence and realization possibilities of A and B and of everyone like them. These cultural things are not only, what H-J. Rheinberger 2001 has called 'epistemic things', i.e. knowledge instruments by which we enlarge, deepen or measure our knowledge horizon, but also everyday artifacts like knife, fork and spoon, recording devices and the whole universe of, what Heidegger 1967 called 'Zeug', tools, vehicles, clothes, furniture, etc. ...

Furthermore C is furnished with all kinds of institutions housing and/or handling education, administration, fabrication, faith, service, habitation etc. tasks. Institutions are again combined and localized in places – working places, living places – and on a second level in villages, and towns. On a third level all these things and places are combined in geographically and/or politically and/or culturally definable countries and states.

It is about time to leave this sketch of the complex reality of my three exemplary conscious beings and to jump into the proper subject of my considerations – social work and the complexity of its logic. In flight and before landing let me say a word about the logic of this complex way of being and self-realizing. I take logic here very broad as thinking resource or, as Aristotle called it, thinking organ. It goes without saying that 'organ' here not only should be understood as the bodily organ of thinking identified with the brain. The brain may be the physic-chemical part of thinking but logic as thinking organ means also the – let's say - mental version of a thinking resource. 'Mental' on its part shouldn't dualistically be understood as incorporeal. I don't believe in a mental substance. In any way it is clear that logic is about how we think and not about how the brain functions. We think in and through linguistic structures, i.e. structures of phonetic or graphic signs. We think also in and through visual structures consisting of color spots. And we think in and through sound sequences and harmonies consisting in air vibrations or graphical signs representing them. Eventually we think in and through actions consisting in body movements or voluntary forbearances of such. In other words I understand thinking in a very broad sense, including its realizing by action. Logic has then to do with the different meaning-constitutive organs and the modus of their manipulation in order to realize our thoughts. In short: logic has to do with the construction and forming of human, i.e. conscious, existence.

In the last moment before my landing in social work issues – I confess that I also take social work not only in the narrow sense of a not specially appreciated and rather bad paid profession but in the broader existential and philosophical sense of conscious life work of self- and society realization. In this broad sense, social work is in my opinion the epitome of what I understand by philosophical work. The crux of this kind of work is that self- and society realization can go wrong. Does it not then its result can be what the Greeks meant by eudemonia – a good, meaningful and ingenious life.

A life can of different reasons go wrong: for instance because of inherited physical or mental handicaps; or because of bad habits – acquired or assumed – or simply because of bad physical, economic, mental or social luck: storms and floods, economic crises, severe diseases, dead of loved persons, unwanted divorces, dismissals from work, crimes and wars, political or religious oppression and terror[2].

Now we have arrived at the real world. In this world, social work is not only part of everyone's striving for an as good as possible personal and social life but a social necessity. It's necessary because of the fact of social need. Social work exists as a profession because modern growth and competition societies couldn't possibly survive without professional social help for the misfits of and losers in such societies. The function of social work in them is to avert the epidemic growth and dispersion of what I will call social diseases. Prototypes of social diseases are all kinds of stress, depression and angst "dispositions" that impede people in being disposed to function in accordance with the societal requests to succeed.

To show at least a small part of the complexity of social work logic let me outline what I will call a social work situation. Using ideas from situation semantics (Barwise & Perry 1999) and situation logic (Barwise 1989, Devlin 1993) I understand a situation as a domain of individuals having properties and relations. These individuals are topologically placed in relation to each other and the whole situation within a

---

2   Dante 2011 has in his Commedia described a universe of things that can go the right and wrong way in human life and history; but at the same time he placed and evaluated the consequences of human action in a both physical and mental cosmos (inferno, purgatorio, and paradiso) in a way that defines, we could say, though in a very questionable way, an overall meaning with human existence. Only few other men have like him dared to arrogate for themselves to deliver a judgement about human and natural history as a whole.

geographic environment. The situation and its elements are also temporally localized regarding the time of the day, of the year, and of history. What is the case and happens in the situation has furthermore its duration and is localized within the overall duration of the situation itself and the universal history.

A social work situation is then more specifically characterized as a three-part interaction between a person needing social help, let's say A, a person willing to give social help, let's say B, and a common consciousness, let's say C. The latter is present in the form of all those artifacts and communal institutions housing and surrounding the interaction of A and B. I am talking about a building, typical a public administration building, a room, typical a social worker office room with corresponding furniture. C is also present in the form of a law corpus defining the rights and obligations both of the person seeking social welfare and of the community affording it, i.e. of A and C. B in her part is as a social worker acting on the basis of a set of rules how to register, to evaluate, and to treat the case of a person seeking social welfare. By the presence of C, B knows in general what she has to do in order to afford or not, what A is seeking to get.

There exists a basic problem in a social work situation grounded in the different position and motivation of A and B as interaction partners on the one hand and their equality as conscious beings on the other hand. Different from other kinds of helping people, social welfare is touching the basic status and constitution of a conscious being equipped with free will. Being able to choose deliberately between alternative possibilities in a given situation and taking the responsibility for one's choice is decisive for the self-confidence and social respectability of a person. The concept of 'good life' is bound to the concept of a free willing and responsible conscious being. If happiness isn't exclusively the result of good luck, i.e. if a human being should be able to influence his or her destiny then it is essential for realizing a good life – in the Greek, eudaimonian sense – to preserve his or her capability of free, self-responsible decision. On this background the basic problem of social work is the risk of making the person seeking social help incapable to realize a good personal and social life that not only depends of good luck. This risk is incorporated in the body of rules and regulations codifying the modes how the social worker as a representative of social consciousness has to proceed in either affording or denying social welfare to the person seeking it.

Nobody is able to know in advance which choices and actions of a conscious being eventually will result in a good or a bad life – neither our exemplary social worker, *B*, nor the social consciousness she represents, nor our person, *A*, seeking social welfare. And this is so because in practical affairs it isn't sufficient to deliberate in the right way and to make the right choices. Only when you also actually have tried to realize your decision you are able to know if it was the right decision. This is identical with the basic problem of ethics. To know the right way to act in a given situation in reference to a wanted end, you not only have to deliberate as well as you can what you think the right action is and to make the right decision how you think you best can realize this action – you have also actually to perform it. This is the basic condition of being conscious: on the one hand consciousness is inseparably constrained to the realization process of all kinds of being but this process is on the other hand contingent, i.e. most probably not completely determined. To be sure, I will not mine here the mysteries of free will and a deterministic or nondeterministic reality.

In any case if we as conscious beings shall be able to cope with a contingent world the constitution of our consciousness must not be delimited and fixed a priori. Only as the result of a continuous interaction between the conscious side and the being side of a conscious being there is a chance for accordance. To be in accordance with or attuned to a changing reality, a conscious being has to dispose of thinking organs like a flexible system of concepts, of predication forms, and modes of inference. 'Flexible' means concerning concepts 'not gridlocked' in rigorous definitions, as Frege requested, and the late Wittgenstein questioned. 'Flexible' means also to realize – as the late Wittgenstein did - that the justification of every system of propositions eventually has to come to an end where it directly encounters reality – i.e. in and through the bodily organs of a conscious being. We are used to call the conscious side of this encounter 'experience'. 'Flexible' means at last also that reasoning not only succeeds in the form of deductive inferences, but always is the result of interplay of multiple inference forms – namely abductive, inductive, transductive etc. inference forms.

Calling 'logic' the "organism" of the conceptual, propositional, and inferential thinking-organs we can resume that a logic that should be able to cope with a complex reality has to be a conceptually flexible, propositionally multivalent[3], and argumentationally multi-inferential logic[4].

To sketch how a flexible conceptualization system could look like I will introduce the notion of a conceptual field. By a 'conceptual field' I mean a dynamic structure of more or less related concepts. Wittgenstein 1963 has called the increasing and decreasing meaning-relatedness between concepts a 'family resemblance'. The dynamic of such meaning fields lies in the fact that concepts not only are representatives for certain entities but at the same time origins of a manifold of more or less similar or different concepts. Every concept is in this way a marker to other concepts and an allusion to alternative possibilities of understanding something. It's like the tonic in music that evokes a series of overtones. Lennart Nørreklit 2008 has taken this field feature of concept-interwovenness as starting point to a philosophical method of reality-construction called *complementary conceptualization*. The method helps to detect possible alternatives to established ways of understanding things and of constructing personal and social reality.

Let me then say a few words about what I mean by propositional multivalence. Classical logic and the biggest part of modern logic are built on the so-called bivalence or tertium non datur principle. It says seemingly only that there are only two truth values or that a proposition at the same time only can be either true or false. In fact it says, however, a lot more. The valence of propositions is inextricably interwoven with our understanding of the concept of meaning. By propositions we explicate the meaning of our concepts, and by concepts on their part we condense our experience and understanding of things. By constraining the meaningful to what either is true or false we ignore that thinking isn't separated from all the other forms and modes of being conscious – sensing, feeling, wishing, desiring etc. If we don't ignore this, then 'meaning' stands not only for the semantic content of linguistic expressions but for everything that makes existence in one or other way meaningful for a conscious being. Besides making something recognizable or understandable, things, states, events, and ac-

---

3   In contrast to the bivalence (tertium non datur) principle of determining the truth value of propositions in traditional logic.

4   In contrast to reducing valid inferences to deductive argumentation in traditional logic.

tions can also have, say, aesthetical, instrumental, or ethical meanings and values for us.

That lastly a complex logic has to incorporate a multiplicity of inferential organs and modes besides deduction becomes clear if we consider the innumerable attempts within the history of logic to complement deductive or knowledge justifying reasoning by inductive, abductive or transductive modes of knowledge extending or innovating reasoning. Part of the history of these attempts is both Plato's dialectics and Aristotle's Topics, Descartes' efforts to develop a logic of discovery, Kant's endeavor to integrate epistemic logic with the logic of action and of feeling, Hegel's dialectics etc. ...

Let me conclusively sketch how I think the complex problems of social work as a profession – to help another person to become able to realize a good life – can be solved. Inspiration can be found in Wittgenstein's idea – or rather method – of language games. The reason why I think Wittgenstein's concept of language game is applicable as an appropriate method to tackle the complex logic of social work is as follows: Language game theory is Wittgenstein's fiction of how it is possible to learn a language without a previous language. By applying language game method (cf. Wittgenstein 1963) to real life situations we can test how we can become able to act and communicate meaningfully in forming our lives. 'Language game' is a kind of learning by doing that doesn't only work for language learning. It can be understood as a technique or an art of learning to act and communicate meaningfully in general. Applying the idea of language games to social work, the problem of this work is then how it can be made possible to learn to realize a good life without having lived a good life before. The central point of the logic of language games is that the meaning and value of those things and instruments the interacting participants use and manipulate is not determined in advance but result of the interaction of all parts – conscious and unconscious – of the interaction. By their interaction the participants have a real chance to detect, create, change or affirm the meaning and value of everything that is constitutive of the situation. Furthermore the participants are as the interacting creators of the situation *meaning* responsible for this outcome. If B in our social work situation for instance doesn't treat A only as a special "case" or "instance" of those rules and regulations C requests her to implement then she doesn't risk to incapacitate A in his striving for a better life. If A in the same situation realizes that B doesn't treat him as the deducible instance of a general rule or premise then it will be probably easier for him to detect his own responsibility of and possibilities to co-determine the course and result of the social work situation.

The conclusion of my considerations in this paper can then be expressed in the following way: if a social work situation - understood as an interaction process between two individuals and a social conscious being, *A, B, and C* – could be performed in a language-game-like manner of complementary conceptualization, propositional multivalence, and multiinferential reasoning then the perhaps most crucial problem of social work – to incapacitate the help seeking person – could be avoided.

References

Barwise Jon 1989, *The Situation in Logic*, Stanford: CSLI-Publications.

Barwise Jon & Perry John 1999, *Situations and Attitudes,* Stanford: CSLI-Publications.

Bohm David 2007, *Wholeness and the Implicate Order*, London and New York: Routledge.

Dante 2011, *Commedia*, In deutscher Prosa von Kurt Flasch, Frankfurt a. M.: S. Fischer Verlag.

Devlin Keith 1993, *Infos und Infone*, Basel/Boston/Berlin: Birkhäuser.

Gell-Mann Murray 1997, The Simple and the Complex, in: Alberts D. S. and Czerwinski T. J., eds. 1997, *Global Politics, and National Security*, Washington D.C.: National Defense University.

Heidegger Martin 1967, *Sein und Zeit,* Tübingen: Max Niemeyer Verlag.

Nørreklit Lennart 2004, Hvad er virkelighed?, in: Christensen J. 2004, *Vidensgrundlag for handlen*, Aalborg: Aalborg Universitetsforlag, p. 25-29.

Nørreklit Lennart 2008, *Kritisk ontologisk konceptualisering*, unpublished seminar paper, November 2008, Aalborg University, Department of Learning and Philosophy.

Rheinberger Hans-Jörg 2001, *Experimentalsysteme und epistemische Dinge*, Göttingen: Wallstein Verlag.

Wittgenstein Ludwig 1963, *Tractatus logico-philosophicus, Tagebücher 1914-1916, Philosophische Untersuchungen*, Frankfurt a. Main: Suhrkamp.

List of authors

Tina Maria Fussenegger, (Mag. Art.), 29-year-old anthropologist and teacher. Study of German Philology, Spanish Studies and Social Anthropology in Vienna (2003-2013). Likes eating cheese and drinking wine.

Lennart Nørreklit, PhD. and Dr. Habil., professor emeritus in philosophy and leadership. Creator of the philosophical foundation for the "Actor Reality Construction" research network. Home Address at Arhus University: http://econ.au.dk/research/research-groups/actor-reality-construction/.

Hans-Jörg Rheinberger studied philosophy and biology at the University of Tübingen and the Free University of Berlin. After academic stations in Berlin, Stanford, Lübeck, and Salzburg, he joined the Max Planck Institute for the History of Science in Berlin in 1996. Since 1997, he is director at the Institute. His books include "Toward a History of Epistemic Things" (1997), "Iterationen" (2005), "An Epistemology of the Concrete" (2010), "On Historicizing Epistemology" (2010), and (together with Staffan Müller-Wille), "A Cultural History of Heredity" (2012).

Gunnar Scott Reinbacher, Gunnar Scott Reinbacher, Associate professor at the Department for Culture and Global Studies. Research coordinator for the research group Interdisciplinary Health Research. Chair for European Sociological Association (ESA), research network 16

(Health and Illness). In Research committee for Center for Ethics at Aalborg University. Publications se, Http://personprofil.aau.dk/109658.

Ole Preben Riis, professor in sociology of religion at University of Agder, Norway, appointed to PhD-school of Religion, Values and Society. Has studied social values, philosophy of science and humanities, methodology and sociology of religion. Recent publications: A Sociology of Religious Emotion (2010) with Woodhead, Lancaster. Latest: Åbne Vinduer (2012).

Michael Springer earned a doctor's degree in Theoretical Physics at the University of Vienna (Austria). Besides publishing several novels and radioplays in Germany, he became an editor for "Spektrum der Wissenschaft", the German version of "Scientific American". There, he contributes a monthly column dealing with a wide array of topics from physics to philosophy of science.

Søren Willert, mag.art. (psych.), associate professor at Institute for Learning and philosophy, Aalborg University. Søren Willert sees himself as a university-based psychological practitioner. Psycho-social helping relationships in their many guises (psychotherapy, supervision, coaching process consultation and facilitation …), and mainly with himself in the helper's role, have served as his research platform. Philosophically speaking, he draws inspiration from pragmatist thinking, and especially the work of George Herbert Mead.

Jörg Zeller, PhD. in philosophy, linguistics and sociology from Freie Universität Berlin, Mag. Art. in German Language and Culture Studies from Aalborg Universitet, associate professor in Applied Philosophy, Institute of Learning and Philosophy, Aalborg Universitet. Research focus on logic of practice and culture, ethics, and reality construction.